You,_____
were born to Succeed, and you will.

Success Is Really Your Birthright!

**P.S.   Free Gift Offer for Our Readers
See Pages 143 & 144**

What People Are Saying About . . .

Success:
It's Your Birthright

CONGRATULATIONS!

SUCCESS:
It's Your Birthright

DISCOVER HOW TO CO-CONTROL

YOUR DESTINY

by

Larry & Denise Adebesin

Success: It's Your Birthright

by **Larry & Denise Adebesin**

Printed in the United States of America 1997

ISBN: 0-9651929-8-9

Published by Enrichment Publishing

Dedication

This book is dedicated to the greater one inside of us all. All we need to do is set him loose and allow him to mold us into the excellent, prosperous and loving men and women we were created to be.

If you are ready for bold, courageous and power-packed living, this book will show you how to break down walls and obstacles that are standing between you and your ultimate **success.**

So Dare to Succeed, It's Your Birthright!

Acknowledgments

Thank you very much for taking the time to read this book. As you will find out, this book is the result of the work and ideas of many people who have come and gone before us, and some who are still living. Some of the people who have had the greatest influence on my life and writing will be easily recognized in the chapter on gratitude. However, there are many more people who have been extremely helpful. To these people I would like to say a great big thank you. It would almost be impossible to mention everyone's name in this short space. What I have chosen to do is to introduce you to some of these people throughout the book by giving you a list of some of their books at the end of various chapters.

I would also like to say a big thank you to the wonderful and enthusiastic members of the Trail Blazers Success T.E.E.A.M., who have given me real life opportunities to prove the soundness of the principles you will be reading.

Next are my parents for giving me the opportunity to reach for my dreams. Thank you dad, thank you mom.

I would also like to say a special thank you to my wonderful and beautiful wife, Denise, for the many hours of work and creative ideas she provided for this book.

And finally I would like to thank God the Father, Jesus Christ, and The Holy Spirit for giving me the opportunity to be part of their family.

LARRY ADEBESIN

Table of Contents

How To Get
The Most From This Book

This book is designed to get you from where you are to where you want to be mentally, physically, socially, emotionally, financially, and spiritually. The following suggestions will help you do just that.

1. **PLAN TO WIN!** Set aside a definite time daily to think, plan, study, and grow rich in all areas of your life.

2. **DECIDE WHAT YOU WANT!** Before you start reading this book, make a list of at least one goal in each of the above areas you would like to achieve. This will help you recognize the principles and ideas that will be most useful in reaching your goals.

3. **PERSONALIZE THIS BOOK!** Pretend as if the authors are speaking to you and you alone.

4. **STUDY THIS BOOK!** Do more than read this book, study it. Read it over and over and over again with a pen and highlighter in hand. Underline the areas that apply to you most.

5. **APPLY THE PRINCIPLES** that address your situation by recognizing, relating, and assimilating those principles.

6. **MEMORIZE KEY PHRASES!** Memorize quotations and key phrases that are meaningful to you. This will help you internalize these principles.

7. **LISTEN TO AUDIOTAPES!** Listen to the audio version of this book. Listening helps you to access a different part of your brain and helps you to retain the information better.

8. **SHARE!** Share these principles with others by conducting and leading a study group. This is a good opportunity to put the Success: It's Your Birthright Action Guide to use.

Go For It . . . You Will Win

What This Book Will Do For You

This book when properly read, understood, and applied, will be to your life what Roto-Rooter is to a clogged faucet. It will help you remove all the obstacles, roadblocks, negative conditioning and influences that might be standing between you and your success. This book will show you how to create the destiny you desire by empowering you to reclaim your dignity as a loving, productive and worthwhile person.

After you've mastered the principles in this book, it will suddenly dawn on you that the key to health, wealth, success, happiness, harmonious human relationships, money and more love is within you and you can start using it right now. You will not need anyone's permission to use this master key.

In this book you will learn:

- How to condition yourself for Total Success.

- How to control your Destiny and live the lifestyle of your dreams.

- How to develop the qualities of Excellence, such as Gratitude, Persistence,

- Commitment, Vision, Dreams, Goals, Enthusiasm and Work.

- How to enhance your health and vitality.

- How to get along with people better.

- How to use love to cure all your past unpleasant memories.

- The four eternal laws of nature that guarantee success in whatever you do.

What Is Success?

Good Question! Success is something very subjective and personal. Success has different meanings for different people. We have come across several tremendous definitions and the ones we think best illustrate our meaning of Success are the following:

"Success is a journey and a destination"
–Author Unknown

"Success is the progressive realization of a worthy purpose"
–Earl Nightingale

"To laugh often and much; to win the respect of intelligent people and the affection of children; to earn the appreciation of honest critics and endure the betrayal of false friends; to appreciate beauty, to find the best in others; to leave the world a bit better, whether by a healthy child, a garden patch or a redeemed social condition; to know even one life has breathed easier because you have lived. This is to have succeeded."
–Ralph Waldo Emerson

"Success is living for God in all areas of life by fully accepting and applying His rules for living as given in the Holy Bible."
–Larry & Denise Adebesin

The Merriam Webster dictionary defines Success as, *"The satisfactory completion of something."*

So here you have it. Come up with your definition of success or adopt one of these. Much success to you!

Part I

Total Success Conditioning

YOU ARE MORE THAN
A CONQUEROR

"I am bigger than anything that can happen to me. All these things, sorrow, misfortune, and sufferings, are outside my door. I am in the house and I have the key."

—Charles Fletcher Lummis

You were born to succeed, in all ways and along all lines. You were created to have dominion over the fish of the sea, the birds of the air and over every living creature. You were designed to rule the earth. There is so much power and potential in you that lies dormant. But, based on the way the majority of people lead lives of quiet desperation, you might challenge the foregoing statement.

No matter who you are or what your condition is, I'm going to challenge you to come on a journey with me. A journey that will turn your mourning into dancing and if you are already dancing, get ready to start shouting. All our lives, most of us have been conditioned to put ourselves down and beat ourselves up. I am going to ask you to muster up all the faith, courage, enthusiasm, and energy you can to believe that success is your birthright. If by the time you finish reading this book, I have not persuaded you to believe and know for a fact that you were Born to Succeed, then you can change your mind.

At the outset I am going to tell you a story that will challenge, encourage, motivate, and inspire you to become the person you were meant to be. To become a dreamer again. To become the person you've always wanted to be. Say this phrase silently to yourself . . . *"The best is yet to come."*

As a matter of fact it will behoove you to make a habit of saying it often, because as you will find out later, thoughts and suggestions are powerful. The story goes like this:

An American Indian tells about a farmer who found an eagle's egg and put it into the nest of a prairie chicken. The eagle hatched with the chicken and grew up with them all of his life. The eagle did everything the prairie chicken did because he thought he was a prairie chicken. He scratched in the dust for seeds and insects to eat. He clucked and cackled like a chicken. The eagle flew only a few feet from the ground like chickens do. The years passed and one day the eagle noticed a magnificent bird soaring in the skies in all of its majesty and glory. The eagle inquired of the prairie chicken next to him. He said, "That's a beautiful creature, what is it?" The chicken responded, "That's an eagle, he's the King of the Sky, and Chief of the Birds, but don't give a thought to flying like that. After all you're just a chicken."

The eagle believed the chicken and died like a prairie chicken. What a sad story. That eagle was designed to rule the sky, but was conditioned to stay earthbound. The key word here is conditioned. You were Born To Succeed, but you've probably been conditioned to live a mediocre unfulfilling life. The story of the eagle is the story of most people. Most people listen to the chickens in the environment, the people who try to tell you what you can and cannot do. The people who are always looking out for your best interest. This book is designed to re-condition you for success, abundance, faith, hope, courage, prosperity and most importantly, to Succeed in whatever you choose to do.

Get A New Blueprint Of Yourself

The very first step toward the process of reconditioning will be for you to make up your mind that you are going to do your own thinking and arrive at your own conclusions based on your findings. Make up your mind not to listen to chickens who are going to try to condition you for mediocrity. Take immediate control of your life, by choosing to associate with thoughts and people that encourage you, build you up, support you and spur you toward the attainment of your dreams. Cut yourself away from average and mediocre people. Break away and blaze your own trail. Sometimes this might be tough. In the story of the magnificent eagle, notice the eagle was soaring by itself. To recondition yourself for success, you will have to go it alone sometimes. But which would you prefer? Would you rather be in the company of chickens and lead a life of quiet desperation or blaze your own trail and go for your dreams?

In the *Bible* we read:

> *"This day I call heaven and earth as witnesses against you. That I have set before you life and death, blessings and curses. Now choose life so that you and your children may live."*
>
> *–Deuteronomy 30:19*

Even God Himself, who created you, cannot choose for you. You will have to take the initiative. Notice that not only does God tell you to choose, He also tells you to choose life.

Choose to Succeed in life. Choose to lead a prosperous, happy, harmonious life. You have the power within you to do that. At this point you might be asking yourself, "If everything is this simple and easy, why aren't more people leading successful lives?" The answer is very simple. It is because of conditioning. By the time you finish reading this book, you will have gained a good understanding of how your brain works and how you can recondition yourself to get any result you want. Remember, **the best is yet to come.** If you ever doubt your ability anytime in the future, I want you to remember the story of that eagle, because it is also the story of you and me. We have so much power that we are not using.

In the following chapters we are going to explore several of the qualities we must develop in order to Succeed in life. Some of these qualities include but are not limited to: Gratitude, Persistence, Commitment, Vision, Enthusiasm, and Work. Right now we shall focus on four universal principles that will give us a better understanding of some laws of nature and as a result, help us better re-condition ourselves for Excellence.

"Man belongs where man wants to go."
–Dr. Von Braun

Recommended Reading:

I Dare You	**William Danforth**
Psycho-Cybernetics	**Maxwell Maltz**
Success: The Glen Bland Method	**Glen Bland**

THE PRINCIPLE OF SOWING AND REAPING

". . . a man reaps what he sows. "

–Galatians 6:7

Ask any right-thinking person the following question, "What does a farmer who sows apple seeds reap at harvest time?" The answer unquestionably will be apples. What about a farmer who sows orange seeds? You guessed right. Most people are familiar with this principle in the natural, but refuse to apply it in the mental and spiritual realms of their lives.

The principle of sowing and reaping is one of the fundamental principles of nature that no court of law on earth can or will ever repeal. It is a principle so basic, so simple, so true, yet so confounding to many. Many people wish for love without realizing that to be loved they themselves must sow seeds of love.

Others wish for peace and harmony, while they engage in criticism and instigating problems of all kinds for others. They do not realize that they are definitely going to reap what they sow; they do not realize that nature plays no favorites; they do not realize that to live peacefully and harmoniously with others they themselves must sow the seeds of peace and harmony.

Still others wish for more money without realizing that to have more money, they themselves must sow seeds of money. To quote Thomas Fuller, *"If thou wouldst keep money, save money; if thou wouldst reap money, sow money. "* Notice that

18

the words, wish and must, have been used consistently in the foregoing examples. The reason for that is simple. Nature plays no favorites. The farmer who wishes to reap apples, but does nothing about actually planting the seeds, will reap nothing. Before nature yields apples, apple seeds must be sown. This is a task that must be done. Action must be taken in the form of planting the seeds before apples are ready to be harvested.

The same principle applies to all other areas of our lives. So quit wishing and start doing, someone might say. Why go through these action steps when there are others who get lucky without doing much? That is an excellent idea. The authors also happen to believe in luck based on the following quotation by Stephen Leacock, *"I am a great believer in luck, and I find the harder I work, the more I have of it."* So if you believe in luck, good luck to you, and do more work for your luck. Action now, please. The bottom line is this: the principle of sowing and reaping is an eternal principle. It was here before we got here, and guess what? It will be here when we are long gone. So why not work with it? It's very simple, whatever you want more of, sow more of it and, you will reap what you sow.

In addition to just sowing, it would be advantageous to you to bless and encourage your seeds before you sow them. By this the authors mean that you sow your seeds with a pleasing positive mental attitude and in a spirit of harmony. By doing this, you can expect a very abundant harvest . . . thirty-, sixty-, and one hundred-fold return. And remember, everything that has life benefits from encouragement. Be consistent, be persistent, be optimistic, in your sowing.

> *"It is the farmer who faithfully plants seeds in the spring, who reaps the harvest in the autumn."*
> —B.C. Forbes

Sow cheerfully and reap bountifully.

Recommended Reading

Motivational Classics - (3 books)	Charles "T" Jones
Think Big	Ben Carson
A Better Way to Live	Og Mandino

THE PRINCIPLE OF THOUGHT
AND ACTION

"A man is what he thinks about all day long."
—Ralph Waldo Emerson

The maxim, *thoughts are things,* is a very popular one. But how many people truly believe it? And of those who say they believe, how many of them consciously use their thoughts to mold and shape the things, conditions, and circumstances they want and desire? To think is to act. Every action, be it spontaneous or consciously planned, is always preceded by thought. The entire universe is made up of space, time, matter, energy, and intelligence. Thoughts and actions are the forces that mold the components of the universe into what you and everyone else sees and calls reality. Thoughts and actions are the creators, makers, shapers and molders of wealth and poverty, health and sickness, sadness and joy, ignorance and enlightenment, evil and good. Thoughts and actions are the forerunners of every change in civilization. With the right thoughts and appropriate actions, man can build for himself paradise on earth.

At this point it is important to explore where thinking takes place as well as who does the thinking. Man is a spiritual being having human experiences. Man is a thinker. Thoughts and actions essentially originate from the mind of man.

So much has been written about the mind of man. But for the benefit of those who are not very familiar with the human mind and the way it operates, we shall give a brief description of the mind's operations. We all have a mind, which possesses two separate distinct characteristics. Each part is capable of independent action under certain circumstances. Their functions are essentially different. The two parts of the mind have been given several names. In this book the authors choose to designate one part as the conscious mind, and the other as the subconscious mind.

The conscious mind is the objective portion of the mind, which takes notice of the world that we call reality. The highest function of the conscious mind is reasoning. It is with the conscious mind that we choose who to marry, where to live, what clothes to wear, what foods to eat, etc. The conscious mind is limited by our five physical senses, namely sight, sound, touch, taste, or smell. The conscious mind is capable of both inductive and deductive reasoning, analysis and synthesis. The conscious mind is the portion of the mind we use to establish our goals and dreams. The conscious mind is the goal setter. It makes the plans, and sets the goals.

The subconscious mind on the other hand is the subjective portion of the mind. The subconscious mind is the seat of the emotions, the creative power and the storehouse of memory. The subconscious mind perceives by intuition. It is the subconscious mind that starts our heartbeat, controls the circulation of our blood, regulates our digestion, assimilation and elimination. It changes the food we eat into tissue, muscle, bone, and blood. It heals our body automatically when we get a cut. It is the portion of the mind responsible for controlling all the vital processes and functions of our body, and is capable of solving all of our problems. The subconscious mind is susceptible to suggestion and capable of deductive reasoning only. The foregoing statement is very important. You will do well to read it again and memorize it. Intensity, emotional power, timing and repetition all play a big role in influencing the subconscious mind by suggestion. The subconscious mind functions best when the conscious mind is in abeyance or a condition of suspended activity, i.e., before, during, or after sleep. The subconscious mind is the goal-getter, it develops the power to get the job done. The differences in people around us are caused by the different ways in which they have trained their conscious minds. Subconsciously there is very little difference between people.

So man is a spiritual being. He is a thinker and he thinks in his mind or heart for, *"As a man thinketh in his heart, so is he."* (Proverbs 23:7) Or you can say that as he thinketh in his mind so he acteth in his environment. Thoughts always precede action. Every action is in itself a cause, which in turn has an effect. Everything in the universe is electromagnetic in nature. The laws of attraction and repulsion operate by means of electro-magnetism whereby like attracts like. Think good thoughts and good actions follow. Think bad thoughts and bad actions follow. The thought is the cause, and the action is the effect. *"Do people pick grapes from thorn bushes, or figs from thistles? Likewise every good tree bears good fruit, but a bad tree bears bad fruit. A good tree cannot bear bad fruit, and a bad tree cannot bear good fruit."* (Matthew 7:16-18)

Thoughts and actions are one. It is impossible for one to be without the other. Look upon your mind as a garden, you are the thinker (gardener) and your thoughts are the seeds that you continually sow. And you will reap the fruits of your thoughts, whether good or bad depending on your habitual thoughts. *"Such as are thy habitual thoughts, such also will be the character of thy mind."* (Marcus Antonius) Now that you know that your subconscious mind is susceptible to suggestion, think noble and Godlike thoughts to and for yourself as well as to and for others. Remember, what we feel we attract, what we imagine we become. The feeling of health produces health, and the feeling of wealth produces wealth.

- ◆ Magnetize your mind by continually sowing positive, optimistic, cheerful, happy, harmonious, loving, caring, and enthusiastic thoughts.

- ◆ Re-Vitalize your mind by thinking thoughts of love, peace, prosperity, wealth, and goodwill to all people everywhere.

♦ Energize your mind by taking action now. Step on the gas. Punch a hole in the sky. Break a leg. Get jet propulsion. Make dust in the world.

♦ Purify your mind by cleansing your consciousness of all feelings of resentment, hate, fear, doubt, cynicism, anger, jealousy, antagonism and like emotional reactions toward yourself and others. These kinds of thoughts are like weeds that keep you from reaping the harvest you truly desire. These kinds of thoughts must be eliminated. They must be replaced by the renewing of your mind.

♦ Transform your mind by thinking on things that are true, noble, right, pure, lovely, admirable, excellent, praiseworthy, harmonious, uplifting, and stimulating. Like a powerful magnetized piece of metal which lifts about twelve times its own weight, attract to yourself the conditions, people, circumstances and thoughts that you want by radiating like thoughts to others. Remember, like attracts like.

William James said, "The greatest discovery of my generation is that human beings can alter their lives by altering their attitudes of mind."

Your thought is the seed as well as the cause. Your action or condition is the fruit as well as the effect. And your mind is the soil. Everything in the universe is electro-magnetic, and like attracts like. Your mind is like the magnet that attracts to you all the conditions and circumstances of your life. It is difficult to accept, but we are where we are and what we are because of our thoughts.

"A man's life is what his thoughts make of it."
–Marcus Aurelius

←——————————————————→

Recommended Reading:

The Power of Your Subconscious Mind   Joseph Murphy

What You Say Is What You Get   Don Gossett

IMAGINATION and REALIZATION

"Imagination is more important than knowledge. "
                                    —Albert Einstein

Now that we know that thoughts are things, and that thoughts and actions are one, we also know that thinking takes place in the mind of man. The curious individual would probably want to know how we think and what faculty of our being we use in thinking. That is a question worthy of an explanation. The answer to this is very simple. As spiritual beings having human experiences, endowed with the power of thought, and creative power, we think in pictures. The creative power of man, also known as the creative imagination, is the faculty used in thinking. A thought in the mind is a picture in the mind. For a word in the mind of one individual to be communicated to the mind of another individual, a word must be spoken or a symbol must be conveyed. This word or symbol must be received and translated into a picture before it has any meaning.

For example, think about the last exciting experience you had, hopefully that was within the last twenty-four hours. As you think about this experience, you are probably focusing inside, seeing pictures of yourself doing something or being with someone or somewhere. Now think about the experience some more. You will have noticed that the moment you read the word "think" you pictured yourself again. Why is that?

Thinking is picturing. In order for you to relate that exciting experience to another individual, you will probably use some words, and the words will in turn be translated into pictures by the other person before any sense can be made of your words.

Since we become what we think about, and what we think is what we picture in our mind, what we picture in our mind is what we act upon. It follows then that as man pictures in his mind, so he becomes in his environment. Imagination equals realization. What you picture or imagine, you become. Control your pictures and you control your actions; control your actions, and your control your destiny. Do more than that. Picture the destiny you want. Picture the realization you desire. Picture or visualize the person you want to become. Visualize yourself doing what you love to do most. Visualize yourself having the things you desire. Visualize the good and beautiful in others and your environment. Do this as often as possible. Repetition is the key. Remember what the sage of Concord, Ralph Waldo Emerson, had to say about thinking, *"A man is what he thinks about all day long."* Do it now. Take a few minutes to invent your future. Do It Now!!!

Since we think in pictures, it follows that a man is what he pictures all day long. How are your pictures right now? Would you really want these pictures to be produced in your life as your experiences? If you don't like them you can change them right now, by changing your thoughts. Most of the time all you will need to do is to think the opposite of the unwanted thought.

"Where there is no vision, the people perish."
                                        –Proverbs 29:18

Visualize for yourself and for others that which is noble, wonderful, and Godlike. What you visualize, you think. Your thoughts are like seeds sown in the ground (your mind). Sow good thoughts, reap good results. Sow bad thoughts, reap bad results.

"The good man brings good things out of the good stored up in him, and the evil man brings evil things out of the evil stored up in him."
                                        –Matthew 12:35

Avoid negative and destructive thoughts about yourself and others at all cost. To think ill of yourself or others is like taking mental poison, which will ultimately rob you of your zest, joy, and creativity. Remember the mind is like the soil, which never refuses any type of seed. It produces according to the seed sown. You are the only thinker in the universe as far as you are concerned. Guard the pictures you permit in your heart. Refuse to tolerate any negative thoughts in your mind.

Learn to forgive. Forgiveness is the greatest revenge. Forgive yourself and others. To refuse to forgive is nothing less than ignorance. To forgive is to give something for. Radiate and give thoughts of love, peace, prosperity, wealth, and good will to all.

> *"Above all else guard your heart, for it is the well spring of life."*
>
> *—Proverbs 4:23*

So guard your heart by making sure the pictures you allow into your mind are the pictures you truly want. Imagine the good you want, long enough, and you will experience it.

> *"Whatever you see on the screen of life was first seen in your mind. If you don't like what you see, change the reel of film, change your attitude, change your thoughts. Change your thoughts and you change your world."*
>
> *—Wally "Famous" Amos*

> *"Imagination rules the world."*
>
> *—Napoleon*

You can rule your world by controlling your imagination. Imagination has the power to protect and clothe ideas, plans and purposes by making them visible on the screen of space. Imagination discards everything unproductive. It creates riches, beauty, harmony, justice, joy, health, happiness, and fulfillment. Imagination tramples lack, repudiates sickness, storms discord, and in their places creates wealth, health and harmony.

"The soul without imagination is what an observatory would be without a telescope."

–Henry Ward Beecher

You are always imagining. When you think about an incident that occurred in the past or an incident that you would like to experience in the future, you do it in pictures. Learn to focus your attention on your visions and ideals and imagine them fulfilled. Imagine the successful outcome of your goals. Pay attention to it consistently until it is taken over by your subconscious mind. Then you are certain to see it manifest in your life. Remember the subconscious mind is capable of deductive reasoning. With the naked eye, you can vividly see only what already exists in the objective world. In the same way, the picture you visualize in your mind's eye already exists in the unseen world of your mind. You need only persist long enough until you turn it into reality.

"To successfully imagine an end result is to joyfully and triumphantly realize it."

–Larry Adebesin

$\longleftrightarrow$

Recommended Reading:

Psycho-Cybernetics	**Maxwell Maltz**
Instant Millionaire	**Mark Fisher**

THE SPOKEN WORD

"Words are the most powerful drugs used by mankind."

—Author Unknown

We have already talked about the fact that we think in pictures, and that we use the spoken word to express those pictures. There has been so much written about the power of the spoken word and its impact on the quality of our lives. Some people refer to the spoken word as confession. Others refer to it as affirmation, self-talk, auto-suggestion and hetero-suggestion. For the purpose of this book, the terms auto-suggestion and hetero-suggestion will be used.

Simply defined, auto-suggestion means suggesting something definite to one's self through the five senses of seeing, feeling, hearing, tasting, and smelling. Unfortunately, the majority of us use this principle negatively because of our negative childhood conditioning and also because of the impute of the environment and people we associate with. Auto-suggestion is a very powerful tool that one can use to shape one's circumstances, condition, and ultimate destiny here on earth. Let the reader bear in mind that the term auto-suggestion as used here is referring to the words, pictures and emotions that dominate our minds. Since we think in pictures and use words as symbols to express these pictures, we shall now concentrate on the power of words themselves. Keep in mind that we are making reference to the spoken word here. That is the word that we speak with our mouths.

Hetero-suggestion on the other hand, is the suggestion other people make to you. Again, most of these are negative, because the purpose of the suggestion other people make is essentially to control or instill fear in us.

Examples of hetero-suggestion are . . .

"You'll never amount to anything."
"You can't do that."
"You are a dreamer."
"Don't do this or else."
"Why try?"
"You're too old, or too young."

. . . and so on and so forth. You might be saying to yourself, "If auto-suggestion is what I say to myself, most of which has been negative, and hetero-suggestion is what others say to me, which is also negative a good share of the time, what chance do I stand to change this?" The answer to this is very simple. Here is why – your conscious mind, or the reasoning part of your mind, has the power to reject the suggestions given by others. In other words you do not have to accept what others say to you. You can reject it by simply saying to yourself, "I reject that statement or comment, and I don't accept it as true for me."

Since your subconscious mind is amenable to suggestion, it follows that you can change the way you talk to yourself and others, starting right now by making sure that the words you speak serve to heal, quicken, vitalize, energize, inspire, motivate, bless and prosper yourself and others. Your words have the power to build or destroy, bless or curse, kill or make alive.

"The words that I speak are spirit and they are life."
                                                    –John 6:63

The *Bible* has many wonderful verses that talk about the power of words. We believe it would be a wonderful idea to explore some of these verses, because they are potent enough to convey the importance of the spoken word to the right thinking person.

"In the beginning was the Word . . . "

—John 1:1

Everything you and I become or do usually begins with the word. You rarely do anything without saying it first. For example you probably said to yourself, "I'm hungry and I'm going to eat now," and then you go and eat. Again, most of the things we do are a result of what we've thought or said.

"Pleasant words are a honeycomb, sweet to the soul and healing to the bones."

—Proverbs 16:24

"From the fruit of his lips a man enjoys good things . . ." and "He who guards his lips guards his life, but he who speaks rashly will come to ruin."

—Proverbs 13: 2-3

Recommended Reading:

The Tongue: A Creative Force   **Charles Capps**

What To Say When You Talk To Yourself   **Shad Helmstetter**

Hung By The Tongue   **Francis Martin**

THE INFLUENCE OF HABIT

"Sow a thought and you reap an act. Sow an act and you reap a habit. Sow a habit and you reap a character. Sow a character and you reap a destiny."
—Author Unknown

You and I are where we are and what we are because of our established habits. In the story of the eagle and prairie chickens, we learned that the eagle was designed to rule the sky, but was conditioned to stay earthbound. Condition is a direct result of habit. Our habits, or conditioning, control our destiny.

Aristotle said it best when he said, "We are what we repeatedly do. Excellence, then is not an act, but a habit."

You see, the people who lead lives of Excellence have formed the habit of doing things that mediocre people don't like to do and won't do.

A habit is a pattern of behavior, which can only be acquired by frequent repetition or consistent practice. Some experts say it usually takes 21-30 days to form a new habit. Most people who lead lives of quiet desperation, do so because of years of negative conditioning. According to Dr. Shad Helmstetter in his book, *What to Say When You Talk To Yourself* (a powerful book that I suggest you read and study), the average person hears the word "No" or "You can't do that," about 148,000 times in his first 18 years. This compared to a few thousand or a few hundred "Yes" or "You can do it," in the same amount of time. Dr. Helmstetter goes on to say that leading behavioral researchers say as much as seventy-seven percent of everything

34

we think is negative, counter-productive and works against us. According to medical researchers, seventy-five percent of all illnesses are self-induced. This negative conditioning has a tendency to form habits of thought that are sometimes difficult to break. These habits in turn create our reality and our destiny.

> *"The beginning of a habit is like an invisible thread, but every time we repeat the act we strengthen the strand, add to it another filament, until it becomes a great cable and binds us irrevocably, thought and act. "*
>
> *—Orison Swett Marden*

Based on the four principles of nature that we've already discussed, you now have an idea of how habits are formed. Habits are formed primarily as a result of our thinking patterns. Those thinking patterns are then manifested in our lives. It is our thinking that determines what we do and don't do. Our thinking patterns are also based on our conditioning. Our dominating conditions cause us to act in different ways at different times.

According to medical researchers and experts in human behavior, here is how it works: every decision we make is based on our dominating thoughts, which could be based on fear or faith. Every decision we make usually produces an action. That action is usually a first cause, which has its own effect, and this causes a chain reaction. If we persist in making similar decisions (similar causes), we will continue to get similar results (effects). If this persists long enough it creates a direction. And if we keep going in a particular direction long enough, we'll create a destiny. Hopefully, the destiny we want.

> *"We first make our habits, and then our habits make us. "*
>
> *—Henry David Thoreau*

For example, if you make a decision today to save ten percent of your income, that decision will cause you to take some specific action. Maybe you'll open a bank account or a mutual fund (cause). This would result in an increase in your net worth (effect). If you persist in doing this for months, you will start creating a financial direction for yourself. Keep the procedure up for some years and before you know it you will have created a stable, secure financial destiny for yourself, all other things being equal.

This same procedure works the same way in all areas of our lives. Most of us understand this simple truth on a superficial level, but we fail to apply it in our lives. What do I mean by this? The average person reading this book will at least agree that, what we are and where we are, are direct results of our thoughts. But when it's time to make some changes in our lives, these same people will want to change the effect and not try to impact the cause. As long as we focus on the effect or the results we are getting in life to the exclusion of the cause, we will always get the same results.

The best way to change our destinies or the direction we are moving toward if we don't like it, is to understand the sequence of how destinies are formed or created. Also, we must realize we can re-condition that sequence if we don't like what we are presently getting. Just like the story of the eagle, you and I have the power to choose our destinies, but we must take personal initiative. We must make a commitment to live the life of Excellence. Here are a few thoughts that further illustrate the immensity of the power we possess. Three of the following quotes are taken from James Allen's classical inspirational book *As A Man Thinketh . . .*

"Mind is the Master that molds and makes, and man is mind, and evermore he takes the tool of thought, and shaping what he wills. Brings forth a thousand joys, a thousand ills: He thinks in secret, and it comes to pass: Environment is but his looking glass."

–James Allen

36

"Man is the master of thought, the molder of character, and maker and shaper of condition, environment, and destiny."

–James Allen

"Every man is where he is by the law of his being; the thoughts which he has built into his character have brought him there, and in the arrangement of his life there is no element of chance, but all is the result of a law which cannot err."

–James Allen

"Things do not change; we change."

–Henry David Thoreau

Part II

Co-Controlling Your Destiny

HOW TO CHANGE YOUR DESTINY

"Jesus said, if you can believe, everything is possible for him who believes."

−Mark 9:23

"I know of no more encouraging fact than the unquestionable ability of man to elevate his life by a conscious endeavor."

−Henry David Thoreau

To change your destiny, there are three main requirements. First, you must accept full responsibility for your present condition. I realize this is a tough one to swallow, but reason with me a little. If it's true that you are responsible for your present condition, and you take the initiative to change, you will be the better for it. If it's not true, you will not have lost anything in the process. However, if it is true and you don't try to improve yourself, no one will suffer more than you. Remember that you and I have been given the power of choice by God. It is up to us to use it.

This same thinking goes for Christians who are always claiming that Jesus Christ is the only way to God. Look at it this way. If Christians are wrong, we have everything to gain and nothing to lose by believing, then everybody gets to God. If we are right and I believe we are, we still have everything to gain, but the unbelievers do not.

The point I'm trying to make is, play it safe, and take responsibility for your life. You can never go wrong by trying to improve your lot in life.

"The price of greatness is responsibility."
—Sir Winston Churchill

Answer these questions.

1. **If you can love your spouse more, should you?**

2. **If you can take better care of your health, should you?**

3. **If you can be a good role model for others, should you?**

4. **If you can improve your life for the better, should you?**

Of course you should. Remember, what God gave you is life. What you give back to Him is your lifestyle. Strive to give Him at least your commitment to improvement. You can do it. Go for it starting now.

"Choice! The Key is Choice. You have options. You need not spend your life wallowing in failure, ignorance, grief, poverty, shame, and self-pity. But, hold on! If this is true, then why have so many among us apparently elected to live in that manner?

"The answer is obvious. Those who live in unhappy failure have never exercised their options for a better way of life. Because they have never been aware that they had any choices." (Taken from *The Choice* by Og Mandino)

I am asking you to choose the life of Excellence. You were born to Succeed. I realize it is not easy, but what else is new? Life is a challenge. You must cut yourself away from the average, the mediocre, and chart your own course to the destiny of your dreams.

"Accept the challenges, so that you may feel the exhilaration of victory."
—General George S. Patton

"To conquer without risk, is to triumph without glory."
—Pierre Corneille

Believe you were born to Succeed. Believe you are a co-creator of your destiny. Believe you can change your destiny for the better.

"They conquer who believe they can."
—Ralph Waldo Emerson

The next thing you must do to change your destiny is to be willing to change. You were born to Succeed, but in order for you to Succeed, you must be willing to do whatever it takes.

"The Spirit, the will to win, and the will to Excel are the things that endure."
—Vince Lombardi

The third thing you must do is understand the sequence of how thoughts become things. In other words, how we go from conditioning to Destiny. So let's begin.

We are going to do this in reverse order. Most people are used to paying attention to the effect alone, but we are going to do more than that. We are going to trace our destiny to its source, the foundation of thought, the essence of our actions. In doing so, we will learn how to change our destinies for the better by influencing the source itself, which is our conditioning or programming as Dr. Shad Helmstetter calls it.

Before we start, it might be appropriate for you to read and reread this quote on habit. It will do a lot to help you take immediate control of your destiny, if you're ready.

The Power of Habit

"I will push you onward or I'll drag you down to failure. I'm at your command.

"Half the tasks that you do, you might just as well turn over to me, and I'll do them quickly and correctly.

"I am easily managed. You must merely be firm with me. Show me exactly how you want something done and after a few lessons, I will do it automatically.

"I am the sermon of all great people, and a lash of all failures, as well. Those who are great, I have made great; and those who are failures, I've made failures.

"I'm not a machine, but I work with all the precision of a machine, plus the intelligence of a person.

"You may run me for profit or run me for ruin – it makes no difference to me.

"Take me, train me and be firm with me, and I'll lay your work at your feet. But be easy with me, and I will destroy you.

"Who am I? Habit is my name."

–Author Unknown

Destiny

Our current position in life right now is the result of certain decisions we've made in the past. If we continue to make decisions the same way we've done in the past, we will continue to get similar results.

Remember our thoughts and feelings create our destiny. Commit to changing the thoughts and ideas that are no longer serving you. Cease doing things the same way and expecting different results.

When your dress is old you change it, when your car gets old you replace it. Why not do the same thing with your thinking patterns? The apostle Paul wrote *". . . when I was a child I talked like a child. When I became a man I put childish ways behind me."* (1 Corinthians 13:11)

Why not take his advice by putting all those ideas, beliefs and thoughts that are no longer serving you, behind you? Get a new vision of yourself. Believe you can rise above your problems and you will.

You were born to overcome. Enjoy God's abundant riches. Don't settle for anything less. Expect the best. Face each day and challenge with faith, courage, and enthusiasm, then watch things change for you. Change your thoughts today and you change your destiny.

Actions

Our actions or behavior have the most visible manifestation of our decisions. Whatever decision we make usually translates itself into some form of action (effect). Because we reap what we sow, it follows that right decisions will produce right actions. Wrong decisions will produce wrong actions. **"A good tree cannot bear bad fruit, and a bad tree cannot bear good fruit."**

For example: Someone who is happy, joyful, zestful and enthusiastic most of the time, probably decides consciously or unconsciously to be that way. Then they back that decision up by smiling, singing, laughing, doing things and taking actions that inevitably lead to happiness, joy, zestfulness, and enthusiasm.

On the other hand someone who is almost always frowning, complaining, tired and lethargic, takes actions that encourage these qualities. If our destiny is a result of our actions, then what makes us act the way we do? Why do we act in ways that empower us sometimes and in ways that disempower us at other times? What causes the change? Why is it that we act against logic and reason sometimes?

Emotions

Our emotions or feelings are responsible for the way we act. How well we approach or don't approach a task has everything to do with the way we feel. Have you ever noticed how nice most people act between Thanksgiving and Christmas? Have you ever asked yourself why? The reason most people act nice during that period is because of the feelings and emotions the holiday season creates.

Let's move ahead a few more months, about four months, around April 15. At tax time, you will notice that most of those same people are now anxious and nasty. Why is that? Well, it's because of the feeling that tax filing creates in most people.

You've probably noticed also in your life experiences that you tend to get better results from your activities when you feel good. And your results are not so good when you feel bad even though the task is the same. What you feel you attract, and what you imagine you become. What causes us to have emotional ups and downs? Why do we wake up some days feeling lousy and yet on other days we are ready to conquer the world?

Attitudes

Our attitudes are the primary cause of our feelings. **Attitude is defined as: the position or bearing as indicating action, feeling or mood.** What an appropriate definition. Notice the words action, feeling and mood.

Our attitudes towards other people, events, or circumstances, determine how we feel, which in turn determines how we act and ultimately create our destiny. Our attitudes, good or bad, originate deep inside us. And it is our attitude toward life, other people, and events that determine resulting attitudes toward us.

Good and bad attitudes are not the result of success and failure. Success and failure are the result of good and bad attitudes. If this is true, then how and where do we get our attitudes?

Paradigms

Our attitudes are a result of our paradigms. The word paradigm is a Greek word that is generally referred to today as a mental map or a model. A paradigm is a way of thinking, a way of seeing things. It's our perception. Our attitudes are influenced by our mental maps (paradigms) and we all have a bunch of maps. Just as in real life, the map does not equal the territory, our paradigms do not equal reality most of the time, but they are attempts to explain reality.

Our paradigms for the most part are our reality, which is the way we see things (our perceptions). Our perceptions of reality are often erroneous. If they were not mostly erroneous, most of us will be working with nature to build and improve our lives instead of against her. The Apostle Paul put it well when he wrote, *"Now we see but a poor reflection as in a mirror, then we shall see face to face. Now I know in part, them I shall know fully, even as I am fully known."* (1 Corinthians 13:12) Most of us have paradigms that are like poor reflections in a mirror because we have partial knowledge of reality. Our attitudes grow out of our paradigms. Therefore, if we want to have good attitudes, we must see things as close to reality as possible. We must know fully, even as we are fully known.

The moment we make a shift in paradigm, a brand new world opens for us. Paradigm shifts, like most other things, can be empowering or disempowering. And whichever they are, they usually have a tremendous impact on our lives. Most of the changes in the world and in our lives have been the result of shifts in paradigm. Think about it. Where do our paradigms come from or how are they created?

Beliefs

Our paradigms are a result of what we believe. A belief is a thought in the mind. The stronger the thought, the stronger the belief. Belief is something personal because it is not based on reason or logic. What you believe does not have to be true, you only have to accept it as true. Belief simply put, is what you have accepted to be true for the moment, because beliefs do change. Belief is something personal. Belief is subjective. Belief is a matter of choice.

"The belief that becomes truth for me . . . is that which allows me the best use of my strength, and the best means of putting my virtues into action."
—*Andre Gide*

"Belief is the power that has no limitations within reason. Belief is the magic that lights up one's life with possibilities. The initiator of all achievement. The hook-up to a power greater than we are."
—*Dale Galloway*

Belief is anything you have chosen to accept as true and real for you, regardless of what evidence might be available to you. Belief is a learned habit. What makes belief so personal is your mind, the power of the human mind.

Whatever you feed your mind repeatedly, whether faith or fear, harmony or discord, prosperity or lack, is going to be the belief of your mind. The human mind is such a powerful organism, that it will create whatever reality you condition it to create (good or bad). The choice is yours. And what you condition your mind to believe, doesn't have to be true. It only

48

requires that you accept it. And that's a choice you have. Not even God can make you believe anything you don't want to believe. That's why Jesus could only do a few miracles in His own hometown, because of the disbelief of the townspeople or lack of acceptance of His power to heal them.

"Jesus said, if you can believe, everything is possible for him who believes."

–Mark 9:23

". . . Your faith has healed you . . ."

–Mark 5:34

Just because beliefs are personal does not mean that everything you believe is right, by no means. It only means it is right for you. And more often than not, what we believe is erroneous, limiting and disempowering, which is why the majority of humanity is in bondage. It will be helpful for the reader to test what he or she believes against eternal verities, just to be sure that your beliefs are in harmony with nature. Here are a few beliefs that will make life more meaningful:

♦ Believe in the law of sowing and reaping (cause and effect).

♦ Believe in the power of your thoughts to create things. (As a man thinketh in his heart so is he.)

♦ Believe that we live in a world of abundance and that any lack we experience is nothing but a lack of faith.

♦ Believe in the greatest commandment, which is, there is only one God and we are to love Him with everything we have, and also to love our neighbors as ourselves.

♦ Believe in everything that will help you live a fuller, happier, more fulfilling life, so long as it does not violate the laws of God and the rights of others.

How does one believe? How does one become a believer of anything (concept, idea, or philosophy)?

Conditioning

Everything you believe is a direct result of what you have been conditioned to believe through words, pictures, environment, television, radio, sermons, newspapers, etc. The *Bible* tells us in Romans 10:17 that faith comes by hearing. And I would like to substitute the word conditioning for faith, because you develop both the same way, by accepting information.

If you listen to people who encourage, inspire, and motivate you to go for your dreams, you develop hope, courage, and optimism. If you listen to people who put you down, who tell you how the world is going to the dogs, you become anxious, fearful, and discouraged.

The difference between you and any other person who is more or less successful than you, is not race, intelligence, education, etc. It is conditioning. Conditioning is not based on reason, but is a result of faith, belief, action, and choice. Conditioning of any kind takes time and effort. Conditioning ourselves to get positive results takes a conscious effort. It requires using our drive, passions, emotions, will power, and persistence.

Our conditioning determines our belief and out of our beliefs our paradigms are formed. Our paradigms in turn create our attitudes, then feelings, actions, and finally our destiny. What causes our conditioning or where does it come from? This is by far the most important question, because the answer holds the key to our ability to have a tremendous and revolutionary impact on our lives.

Unfortunately the answer to this question is not simple because there are many factors that affect our condition. The good news is that we have a lot of control over what we choose to expose our minds to.

Again we come back to the power of choice. We can not directly affect everything that conditions our minds, but we can indirectly control our destiny by choosing appropriately.

Choice

What you choose to believe and act on is your personal choice. Regardless of the environment or external influence or pressure, you can always choose to believe what you want. Remember: **Destiny is not a matter of chance, but of choice.** You've probably also heard the phrase that says, **"It's not what happens to you that matters, but how you choose to respond."**

Choice then is the main source of our conditioning. We will now take a brief moment to focus on some things we can choose to do to control our destiny.

Thoughts

Throughout the ages, wise men, philosophers, religionists and all right-thinking men and women have all agreed that we are a product of our thoughts. The ancient King Solomon said, *"Above all else guard your heart, for it is the well spring of life."* (Proverbs 4:23)

Emerson said, *"A man is what he thinks about all day long."*

Marcus Aurelius said, *"A man's life is what his thoughts make of it."* He also said, *"Such as thy habitual thoughts, so also will be the character of thy mind, for the soul is dyed by thoughts."*

James Allen said, *"As we think, so we are. As we continue to think, so we remain."*

James Allen also said, *"We are what we think. All that we are arises with our thoughts. With our thoughts we make our world."* Since we become what we think, it will help us very much to think thoughts that are true, noble, right, pure, lovely, admirable, excellent, and praiseworthy as the Apostle Paul admonished us in Philippians 4:8. Every action we take is preceded by a thought so it follows that if we can control our thoughts we can indirectly influence our destiny.

Words

The words we speak have the power to manifest or clothe themselves in physical reality. Words are so powerful because they help us develop faith. Jesus said, *"Out of the abundance of the heart, the mouth speaks."* Words are like containers, they can carry faith or fear, love or hate, according to our choice. Faith comes by hearing. Hopefully you are getting the secret of conditioning.

You see, when we think a thought, the thought resides in our hearts. If we think a thought long enough, it becomes abundant in our hearts, and out of the abundance of the heart the mouth speaks. When the mouth speaks it, the ears hear it, and more faith for that thought comes and goes into the heart again and the cycle continues.

Faith is belief in action. The words faith, hope, and belief all work hand in hand in helping us condition ourselves. Faith is belief of the mind. Faith is a state of mind. *"Faith is the substance of things hoped for, the evidence of things not seen."* (Hebrews 11:1)

Unfortunately for us this law of nature and conditioning is not partial. It works for both positive and negative thoughts. And I say unfortunately because experts tell us that about 77% of the average person's thoughts are negative.

The good news is that we can choose to change that right now by exercising our power of choice. The simplest, easiest and quickest way to do that is by changing either our thoughts or the words we use immediately, if they are not empowering.

Changing our thoughts is a lot simpler than most people would like to believe. The challenge is that it requires eternal vigilance and persistence to do a good job. And most people are just not willing to keep on keeping on until they win.

Remember you were born to Succeed. So don't give up the fight. Fight for your destiny. You were born to Succeed. You have what it takes, so do it and do not quit. Look your fears and doubts in the face and lick them and say with the great motivator Les Brown, *"It's not over until I win."*

Our emotions are not always subject to reason, but they are subject to action. Action puts all fears and doubts to flight. When a negative thought comes to your mind, counter it by saying something positive aloud. Of course you want to do this when you are alone or in the company of those who support you.

Our mind is like a cassette tape which has a message recorded on it. You could do one of two things if you don't like the message: record a new message or throw it away and get a new one. Of course, you can't get a new mind, but you can renew the one you have by recording good desirable thoughts over the bad tape. That's how the mind works. The moment you catch yourself thinking a negative thought, push your mental stop button and record over it. I realize this requires a lot of discipline, but believe me it's worth it. After all it's your life. It's your destiny.

Renewing your mind requires a great deal of concentration, but anything in life that is worthwhile does. As Emerson put it, *"Concentration is the secret of strength in politics, in war, in trade. In short, in all management of human affairs."*

Mental Pictures

The next area of conditioning we can choose to influence is our mental pictures. As we've already mentioned we, as humans, think in pictures not in words. For example when I say the word *car* you probably don't see the letters C-A-R, you probably see the picture of a particular car in its full detail and with color.

Since we think in pictures, why not create an ideal picture of how you will want your life to be? See yourself doing what you'll love to do most, and being with the people you would love to be with. See yourself having the things you desire, feeling the way the ideal you will feel. Do It Now! Now, hold this picture constantly before you. Before you know it, you will become that person.

Another reason why you need to create a picture of your ideal self is so that you can focus on it when a negative thought pops into your mind. It works like this: when a negative thought pops into your mind, push your mental stop button again, then record the picture of the ideal you over that negative thought. By choosing to attack these negative thoughts, words and feelings at all levels, you will eventually win out and become the person you've always wanted to be. Just keep on keeping on. You deserve your dreams.

"Imagination governs the world." (Benjamin Disraeli) And your imagination will govern your ideal world too, especially if you choose to let it govern your world by choice, your choice. Get a good image of yourself. See yourself the way God sees you. *"What things so ever ye desire, when you pray believe ye have received them and ye shall have them."* (Mark 11:24)

The foregoing statement by Jesus is the essence of forming good mental pictures. In order for you to believe you will receive what you pray for, you must continually visualize it. You must continue to imagine it in your mind's eye. Imagination equals realization. Athletes do this all the time. All professionals in all walks of life do it, so why don't you do it as well? The concept is very simple; before you can win in real life, you must expect to win in your mind. In other words, it must happen for you within, before it can happen without. The following is a classical example: Several years ago the University of Chicago conducted an experiment. Students with the same ability to play basketball were divided into three groups and asked to shoot foul shots. Their initial results were recorded. Each of the three groups were then given very special instructions. They were as follows:

♦ The first group was told not to practice playing basketball for 30 days.

♦ The second group was instructed to practice shooting foul shots every day for 30 days for one hour daily.

♦ The third group was instructed not to go to the basketball court for 30 days. Instead they were to practice shooting foul shots in their heads (mentally) for an hour daily.

After 30 days, the students' results were recorded again. As one would expect, the first group – who did not practice at all – showed no improvement. The second group – who practiced as usual on the court – increased their results by twenty-four percent. The third group – who did not even set their feet on the court, but who had only practiced in their heads – made an outstanding 23% improvement. Almost the same as those who actually played the game. This goes to confirm the point we have been trying to make all along.

Imagination equals realization. It also confirms the findings of Dr. Maxwell Maltz. "Experimental and Clinical Psychologists have proved beyond a shadow of doubt that the human nervous system cannot tell the difference between an actual experience and an experience imagined vividly and in detail." Why not put this simple technique to use in your life? Do it now, it will make a difference in your life.

Questions

Questions are next on the list of choices we can make to create a forceful, convincing, empowering impact on our destiny.

> *"He who asks questions cannot avoid the answers."*
> —*Cameroon Proverb*

The questions we ask, particularly the ones we ask ourselves can condition us for fear or faith, failure or success, sadness or happiness. Remember as we think, so we are. If you ask yourself positive questions, you are probably going to get positive answers. If you ask yourself disempowering questions, you are probably going to get disempowering answers.

For example, let's say you just made a big mistake. You did something really stupid. Upon evaluation of the incident you could ask yourself a question like, "Why do I always make this stupid mistake?"

He who ask questions cannot avoid the answers, since the mind is trained to give you answers to whatever questions you ask it. Your mind is probably going to go back into your experiences to look for reasons why you always make stupid mistakes. Now this answer will be recorded into your mind, and you'll develop more faith for the mistake and keep on making the same mistake.

On the other hand suppose you ask yourself another question concerning the same incident, such as, "How can I learn from this mistake?" Your mind will probably give you answers that will help you turn your mistake into a victory. New doors of possibilities will open for you. The key thing to remember about questions is to form the habit of asking *how* questions instead of *why* questions. *How* questions create possibilities. *Why* questions create limitations.

Associations

The people you associate with can influence your destiny for better or for worse. Therefore as much as you can, you must choose to associate with people who will help you reach your goals. Ask yourself right now, "If you continue to maintain the associations you have now for the next few years, will they help you reach your goals on target?" If the answer is yes, you are on the right track. Keep up the good work. If the answer is no, or you're not sure, you're headed for trouble. Change your associations really fast, or you may end up where you don't want to go.

As the Apostle Paul admonished us in 1 Corinthians 15:33 *"Do not be misled: Bad company corrupts good character."* And the flip side of the story was given to us by the wise ancient King Solomon in Proverbs 13:20: *"He who walks with the wise grows wise. "* Then he goes on to say, *"A companion of fools suffers harm. "* Let's all heed his advice and choose our associations with care based on our ultimate destiny.

Body Language

The way we use our bodies, believe it or not, has a lot to do with our destiny. Communication experts tell us that 93% of our communication is non-verbal, and only seven percent is verbal. Of the 93%, 38% is based on our voice inflection and the other 55% represents our body language.

This is powerful information because our mind communicates with the parts of our body directly. Just as the repetition of negative thoughts manifests itself in negative actions, the repetition of negative, slow, sluggish, body movements, and voice inflection, will manifest itself in our mind as negative energy. This will in turn affect our conditioning, which colors our beliefs. Since our beliefs create paradigms, which in turn create our feelings, which affect our actions, and ultimately control our destiny, we will end up where we don't want to be.

So recondition your mind by putting some enthusiasm in your body language, voice inflection and words. Choose to smile, sing. Move briskly with your head held high. You were born to Succeed. Why not act like it? Even God wants you to walk with your head held high (see Leviticus 26:13). He wants His praise in your mouth (Psalms 34:1-2). Picture the ideal you, full of energy, exuberance, vitality, confidence, and having a pleasing friendly disposition. Then start moving your body the way the ideal you will move.

Information

The books we read, the tapes we listen to and watch, all help to re-condition us for success. I will be referring to all means of information as books for simplicity purposes. But everything I say about books applies to audio and videotapes, compact discs, sermons, speeches, etc. Since we are conditioned by what we see through reading or hear by listening repeatedly, I have become a fanatic when it comes to reading. I can personally tell you that my life has been enhanced and is being enhanced daily because of books.

I love books so much that I decided to become a book broker, so I can have unlimited access to the greatest minds. If you will like to have a catalog of our books, see the back of this book for additional information. I think you will find our selection of over 1,000 titles of books, tapes and videos, etc., life-enriching. Now for some more quotes. Just in case you are concerned about my excessive use of quotes, the first two are specifically for you.

"I quote others only in order to better express myself."
—Montaigne

"Next to the originator of a good sentence is the first quoter of it."

–Emerson

To better persuade you of the importance of reading, I have selected the following quotes. Read and meditate on them.

"You are the same today as you'll be in five years, except for two things, the people you meet and the books you read."

–Charles T. Jones

Interesting, people and books, association and information.

"The average person doesn't read a book a year. That's why he is an average person."

–Anonymous

Wonder what will happen to an average car if the oil were changed less than once a year?

"A man's reading program should be as carefully planned as his daily diet, for that too is food without which he cannot grow mentally."

–Andrew Carnegie

Suppose your mind was your body and you fed your body the way you now feed your mind. Will you be properly nourished or malnourished?

"Books have meant to my life what the sun has meant to planet Earth."
—Earl Nightingale

That probably explains why so many people are without zest and enthusiasm.

"The quickest and best way to enrich your life is to enrich your experiences. The best way to enrich your experiences is by reading and listening to good, life-enriching books and tapes."
—Larry Adebesin

Books and tapes – superhighway to an enriched life?

"There is more treasure in books than in all the pirates' loot on Treasure Island and best of all you can enjoy these riches every day of your life."
—Walt Disney

No wonder he created Disney World.

"He who knows how to read, but does not read is no better than he who cannot read."

—*Unknown*

W-O-W!!!

Are you a serious Leader?

"Leaders are readers. Not all readers are leaders, but all leaders are readers."

—*Charles Jones*

"Do not let this book of the law depart from your mouth. Meditate on it day and night so that you may be careful to do what is written in it, then you will be prosperous and successful."

—*Joshua 1:8*

God, Book, You, Prosperity and Success? Hmmm!!!!!

Talking about prosperity and Success, check this out. Library cards are free. Guess what percentage of the population has library cards? You guessed right . . . three percent. According to the Social Security Administration, of every 100 people who reach age 65, what percentage do you think are financially successful? You guessed right . . . three percent. Is this a coincidence? Three percent with library cards and three percent who are financially successful. Maybe not the same three percent in both groups, but it's still interesting.

According to a recent survey:

80% of the population do not buy or read a book.

70% have not been in the bookstore in the past five years.

58% never read another book after graduating from school.

The average person reads less than one non-fiction book per year.

I once heard Jim Rohn, the Dean of Personal Development, say, "The average home worth $250,000 has a room in it designated Library."

Stunning thoughts and statistics about reading. I wonder if we really need all the social programs we have. I wonder if we are not working on the wrong things. The effects of our neglect to choose our destiny, instead of the cause of our conditioning. I wonder how many people we can get off of welfare if we can persuade them to read and grow rich in all ways. I wonder how many people we can get off drugs by educating them on the negative impact of drugs on society and re-conditioning them to take charge of their lives. I wonder how much violence we can eliminate. I wonder!

I wonder what you, my friend, will do about your reading program from now on. I wonder! I wonder how much more fulfilling and enriching your life will be 90 days from now, if you read a good book for 30 minutes daily between now and then. I wonder! I wonder what your health will be like one year from now if you read one good health and nutrition book every quarter. I wonder!

I wonder what your business will look like two years from now if you read one book on your profession or business once every quarter. I wonder! I wonder what your relationships will be like if you read one book on building good relationships once every six months. I wonder! I truly wonder what your whole life will be like 30 days from today if you read your *Bible* daily for the next 30 days. I wonder! I wonder if you can see what I see, as far as the potential in reading good books is concerned. I wonder!

Whether or not you can see what I see, I am challenging you right now to get on a reading program. Choose to influence your destiny for the better by choosing to re-condition yourself for success through reading. Start reading one of those books you bought a while ago that you have not read.

If you don't have any books, start your own Personal Enrichment Library by ordering our **"Read And Grow Rich"** winners program. See the back of this book for more information if you need some assistance.

The choice is yours. You can change your destiny.

"I know of no more encouraging fact than the unquestionable ability of man to elevate his life by a conscious endeavor."
–Henry David Thoreau

You can consciously influence your destiny. The procedure is very simple. It starts with your choice.

- ♦ Your choices create your conditioning.

- ♦ Your conditioning creates your beliefs.

- ♦ Your beliefs create your paradigms.

- ♦ Your paradigms create your attitudes.

- ♦ Your attitudes create your emotions.

- ♦ Your emotions create your actions.

- ♦ Your actions create your Destiny.

You now have the key.

"I am bigger than anything that can happen to me. All these things, sorrow, misfortune, and suffering, are outside my door. I am in the house and I have the key.
                                                    —C.F. Lummis

You were born to Succeed, it's your birthright. The key is simple. Make a list of the things you want to change in your life. Then ask yourself what you would like the result to be if it were perfect. Write the description of your answer down, then repeat these statements to yourself over and over again with words, pictures, and emotions. You can record them on a cassette tape if you like. This is the art and science of reconditioning yourself for success physically, mentally, socially, financially, and emotionally.

Recommended Reading:

As A Man Thinketh	**James Allen**
7 Strategies for Wealth & Happiness	**Jim Rohn**
Success, Motivation & Scriptures	**William H. Cook**
Man's Search for Meaning	**Viktor Frankl**
The Holy Bible	

Part III

Qualities of Excellence

The following chapters will reveal some of the qualities we must develop in order to Succeed in life. Notice I said develop. These qualities are already part of each and every one of us, but most people have been conditioned to believe otherwise.

Gratitude

"O Lord who lends me life, lend me a heart complete with thankfulness."
                                        —William Shakespeare

Someone once said that an attitude of gratitude attracts more blessings, and how true. Knowing what we know about how the mind operates, it is easy to see why. Whatever we focus on expands; therefore, if we focus on giving thanks for what we already possess, we will attract more blessing to ourselves.

All of us have lots of things we can be thankful and grateful for. The fact that we were born to Succeed is something we all must be grateful for even if we don't fully experience success in our lives. The fact that you are able to read these words is something to be grateful for. And consider your health, your family, your nation, your problems that could be worse that are developing your character, your occupation, etc. There is not one person reading this book who cannot find something to be grateful for.

"We should give thanks that we were born."
                                        —Henry David Thoreau

Give thanks for whatever it is, right now. Plant it as a seed, then nourish it, water it and expose it to sunlight by focusing on it with a thankful heart and watch it grow. One of the greatest sins of mankind is ingratitude. We are always looking for something more, always thinking that the grass is greener on the other side. This reminds me of the stories brilliantly narrated in *Acres of Diamonds* by Russell Conwell. If you haven't read that book lately, I suggest you do so. It will do so much to help you realize that we all have a lot to be thankful for, if we will only slow down and pay attention to our surroundings.

The ancient Psalmist King David, told us to, "Enter God's gates with thanksgiving and His courts with praise; to give thanks to Him and praise His name. (Psalms 100:4)

I wonder why he said that!! Develop the habit of being thankful and grateful and watch wonders multiply in your life.

> *"Praise and gratitude do not move God or the law, but it brings about a transformation in our mind and heart and becomes a spiritual and mental magnet attracting all kinds of good, including money, to us from countless sources."*
>
> *–Dr. Joseph Murphy*

Personally we have so much to be grateful for.

First and foremost we want to take this opportunity to thank God the Father for sending His one and only Son Jesus Christ to die for our sins. This alone is more than sufficient reason for us to be grateful forever.

As you know, we have spent the greater part of this book encouraging and challenging you to develop your mental and spiritual powers. Because of this we would like to acknowledge some of the many men and women who have served as God's channels to influence our lives for the better. We have yet to meet some of these people.

♦ Dr. Jide Iwarere (Howard University Prof. of Finance) for his patience, and desire to lead me to Jesus Christ when I was a student of his. (Larry)

68

- Pastor Michael Sprague (Pastor of Evangelism at Forcey Memorial Church, Silver Spring, MD) for his commitment, desire, and willingness to help me become an informed Christian and for all the time he took to disciple me when I first became a follower of Jesus Christ. (Larry)

- Dr. Dennis Waitely (author, lecturer, and Personal Development Coach) for all the inspiration and wisdom he shared in his audiocassette program **The Psychology of Winning.** I first got hold of his teaching in May 1987, and my life has never been the same. (Larry)

- Mr. Charles "Tremendous" Jones (author, lecturer, Personal Development Coach) for his love for Jesus Christ, his zeal, enthusiasm, and for his great thoughts on the benefit of reading good books as narrated in his book *Life is Tremendous.*

- Dr. Howard Hendrick (Dallas Theological Seminary Professor) for his fresh and humorous way of making Biblical concepts and ideas easy for ordinary people like me to grasp.

- Dr. Frederick K. C. Price (Pastor, Crenshaw Christian Center in Los Angeles, CA) for his faith, courage, and his incredible ability to help any serious person lift up his sights and become the person God created him to be.

- Dr. Mike Murdock (Evangelist, Author and Musician) for challenging us in November 1993 to write a book while we attended his School of Wisdom seminar. The challenge has been met. Thank you for the encouragement and for being an excellent teacher.

- Mr. Jim Rohn (author, speaker, and Business Philosopher) for his ability to challenge, encourage, and inspire us to become better people.

- Rev. Kenneth Hagin (*Bible* Teacher) for teaching us how to develop biblical faith, and for his boldness, courage and willingness to stand for what he believes.

- Napoleon Hill (author and philosopher) for the priceless teachings he compiled and organized into **P.M.A. Science of Success** course, which I still refer to constantly. (Larry)

- Dr. Myles Monroe (Pastor, Author, Teacher) through his books and teachings has helped me to discover my purpose and develop my potential. (Denise)

- Zig Ziglar (Author, Speaker, Entrepreneur) For his sincere concern and thorough review of the original edition of this book and for his non-compromising commitment and conviction to the Christian faith. Thank you for all the recommendations.

- Pastor Turnel Nelson (Apostle, Pastor, Bishop, Our father in the spirit) for all the spiritual guidance and tremendously deep truths revealed from the Word of God.

- Mr. Mike Autry (A Very Special Friend) for giving us tremendous support and assistance many, many years before we ever thought of writing a book.

- Pastors Timothy and Robin Seay (Pastors of Emmanuel Covenant Church in Hyattsville, MD). These are our Pastors and we want to thank them for giving us **REAL** spiritual food to feed on every week.

- Our wonderful parents for their love and support. (Mrs. Lelia Bennett and the late Fred E. Bennett Jr., Chief Adebesin and Mrs. Tola Adebesin)

These are by no means the only teachers we've have had, but they are the ones who have influenced us the most personally. Some of the other great people we've also learned from and still are learning from include: The late Og Mandino, Les Brown, Dr. Joseph Murphy, Anthony Robbins, Pastor Joyce Meyers, Tom "Big Al" Schreiter, Brian Tracy, Randy Ward, Edwin Lewis Cole, Jay Abraham, Oprah Winfrey, Michael Jordan, Joseph Marino, Dr. C.R. Krishnamoorthy, Alan Reid, Dexter

Yeager, our many business associates especially those with the **TRAIL BLAZERS SUCCESS T.E.E.A.M., friends, family members,** and the list goes on. Thank you all very much for all your support.

Recommended Reading:

There's Dynamite in Praise	**Don Gossett**
Acres of Diamonds	**Russell Conwell**

Persistence

"Where there's a will, there's a way."

—Aesop

Lack of persistence is the main reason why those who claim they have heard all these before, fail to get the results they want. On a personal note, I think if I were to rank all of the qualities and attributes of success in life, I will have to rank persistence as numbers one, two, and three.

Persistence is what separates winners from losers. Persistence, when coupled with proper preparation and belief in one's ability to do a thing, is by far the ultimate key to achievement in any walk of life. Former President Calvin Coolidge said it well:

"Press On. Nothing in the world can take the place of persistence. Talent will not: Nothing is more common than unsuccessful men with talent. Genius will not: Unrewarded genius is almost a proverb. Education will not: The world is full of educated derelicts. Persistence and determination alone are omnipotent. The slogan press on has solved and always will solve the problems of the human race."

Never give up. Be persistent, even in the face of insurmountable difficulty, heartache, sorrow, adversity, and opposition. Keep on keeping on.

"Persistent people begin their success where others end in failure."

—Edward Eggleston

That should be a clue to remind you to:

Never Give Up. Be persistent even in the face of insurmountable difficulty, heartache, sorrow, adversity, and opposition. Keep on keeping on.

> *"The conditions of conquest are always easy. We have but to toil awhile, endure awhile, believe always, and never turn back."*
>
> *—Simms*

Get the picture of your ideal destiny. Keep it before your eyes and go for it with the trenchant zeal of a crusader, backed by everlasting persistence.

Never Give Up. Be persistent even in the face of insurmountable difficulty, heartache, sorrow, adversity and opposition. Keep on keeping on.

Why be persistent anyway? That's a good question and the answer lies in the fact that the majority of people are spineless weaklings who don't even try anything one time before they give up. Most people are like the timid feeders in the lagoon who never venture into the deep sea beyond. But you my friend, reading this book, are different, and must continue to dare to be different.

> *"There comes a time in every man's life when he realizes that envy is ignorance, and imitation is suicide . . ."*
>
> *—Emerson*

I'm not saying any of this information I'm sharing with you is something you can master overnight. All I'm suggesting is that we must try to improve ourselves as long as we have the breath of life in us.

> *"So do not throw away your confidence; it will be richly rewarded. You need to persevere so that when*

you have done the will of God, you will receive what he has promised. For in just a little while He who is coming will come and not delay. But my righteous one will live by faith. And if he shrinks back, I will not be pleased with him. But we are not of those who shrink back and are destroyed, but of those who believe and are saved. "

—Hebrews 10:35-39

Wow!!! I hope you get the full impact of the preceding verse. I have it memorized and every time I meditate on it, joy, faith, confidence, the will to do, and the will to keep on keeping on in the face of adversity, leap up from my heart. My bones burn and my heart is full of faith. I pray this verse blesses you as it does me. Better yet, I hope you are one of those who believes and are saved. Remember, *You need to persevere so that you will receive.* Those who persevere, those who persist in the face of adversity or opposition always receive the object of their goal, and so will you if you persist long enough.

Christopher Columbus persisted in sailing through an uncharted portion of the Atlantic Ocean until his persistence helped him discover the Americas.

Persistent people always receive.

Signor Marconi persisted in his search to transport the vibrations of sound with ether, using a wireless means of communication until his persistence blessed the world with its first wireless means of communication. Signor Marconi faced a lot of opposition from his relatives who dubbed him insane and went as far as having him examined in a mental institution. But he pulled through with his persistence and so will you.

Persistent people always receive.

Thomas Edison persisted in his endeavor to perfect the incandescent electric lamp, despite the fact that he failed thousands of times, until he got the combination he was searching for.

Persistent people always receive.

Helen Keller persisted in her attempt to learn to talk despite her inability to speak, see and hear until her persistence won the day. Incidentally Helen Keller also said that, *"Life is a daring adventure or nothing."*

Persistent people always receive.

Dr. Roger Bannister persisted in his pursuit of a strategy to break the four-minute mile, until his persistence triumphed despite the fact no one had ever done such a thing before. Persistent people are trailblazers, they are pathfinders, they are the makers and shapers of progress. They are the movers and shakers of civilizations. They are pioneers, dreamers, goal-setters, men and women of faith, of knowledge who plan methodically and act boldly based on their own beliefs and personal initiative.

Persistent people always receive.

Orville and Wilbur Wright persisted in the development of the airplane, despite the fact that some critics urged them not to try. People were saying that if God wanted man to fly, He would have given man wings. The Wright brothers believed differently, and acted differently until their relentless effort gave us the first airplane.

Persistent people always receive.

Madame Schumann-Heink persisted in her desire to become a great opera singer. She defied the advice of her singing teacher who advised her to pursue a career as a seamstress. Her persistence gave her the desire of her heart.

Persistent people always receive.

Walt Disney persisted in his pursuit of building a truly great amusement park where people would pay to come in and have fun, despite the fact that critics told him he would be lucky if he could get anyone to pay an entrance fee, until his persistence paid off. Now people from all over the world come in throngs to pay big bucks to visit the many Disney creations.

Persistent people always receive.

Nelson Mandela persisted in his belief to rid South Africa of apartheid, in spite of the fact that he was imprisoned for about 27 years, until his persistence made him the first president of democratic South Africa.

Persistent people always receive.

You too, my dear friend, persisted in your quest to walk despite the fact that you fell on the floor, hit your head against the wall and hurt yourself in many other ways until walking finally became second nature to you.

If you drive, swim, speak, sing, type, cook or do anything well, chances are you persisted in the pursuit of that thing. Excellence in all walks of life is achieved through persistence, belief, accurate planning, and action, backed by persistence, more action, and more persistence and more action until you reach your goal.

For your persistence to help you receive, it must be based on what you believe, and what you believe should not violate the laws of God and the rights of people. Fight until – Persist until – Believe until . . .

> *"Nothing can resist a will which will stake even its existence against a stated purpose."*
> *–Benjamin Disraeli*

> *"Fight the good fight of faith."*
> *1 Timothy 6:12*

Fight for what you believe until you receive. Here are a few words of encouragement for you.

"I hold a doctrine, to which I owe not much, indeed, but all the little I ever had, namely, that with ordinary talent and extraordinary perseverance all things are attainable."

–T. F. Buxton

"Persistence conquers all."

–Anonymous

The law of persistence is the law of life, and the law of nature. Nature never deviates from her laws.

"The river seeking for the sea, confronts the dam and precipice, yet knows it cannot fail or miss."

–Ella Wheeler Wilcox

You are a part of nature and if you don't give up, nature will not.

"Great works are performed not by strength, but by perseverance."

–Samuel Johnson

"When you get into a tight place and everything goes against you, until it seems as though you could not hold a minute longer, never give up then, for that is just the place and time that the tide will turn."

–Harriet Beecher Stowe

People with persistence are rare. According to a recent survey of sales persistence:

- ♦ 80% of all new sales are made after the fifth call to the same prospect.

- ♦ 48% of all sales persons make one call and then cross off the prospect.

- 25% quit after the second call.

- 12% call three times and then quit.

- 10% of all salespeople keep calling until they succeed. These are the highest paid people in the country.

Persistence, when engaged in correctly for a worthwhile cause that benefits an individual, and in no way harms society, always pays. Persistence is the law of nature.

Start developing the habit of persistence by memorizing all or some of these quotes. Here's what will happen if you do . . . a few days, weeks, or months from now, you will see yourself, accomplishing more, having more courage, being more confident of your ability to shape your destiny. Society and the environment will start loosing its hold on you until you will finally be able to look at those things and events that used to scare you in a different light. Your paradigm will shift. You will see yourself becoming the person you've always wanted to be, the gentle, bold, and courageous person God created you to be. The next quality we must develop to Succeed in life is commitment.

Recommended Reading:

The Greatest Salesman In The World	**Og Mandino**
The Go Getter	**Peter B. Kyne**
Tough Times Never Last But Tough People Do	**Robert Schuller**

Commitment

Commitment simply means doing what you promised to do when you promised to do it, regardless of feelings, environment or circumstances.

To one degree or another, we all lack commitment from time to time. What we all need to learn, is to become more committed to whatever we set out to do. You are going to find this a very short chapter for the simple fact that at the end of the day, no matter what we are attempting to do, excuses will not cut it. At the end of the day, the world wants to know only one thing. Did you accomplish what you set out to do? The Sherson Lehman Brothers put it well:

"Commitment is the stuff character is made of, the power to change the face of things. It is the daily triumph of integrity over skepticism."

You and I need to learn to triumph over the skepticism of other people who will try to rain on our parade. We need to commit to our goals, dreams, and desires, and let everything else go.

Johann Wolfgang von Goethe's version goes like this:

"Until one is committed there is always hesitancy, the chance to draw back, always ineffectiveness. Concerning all acts of initiative and creation, there is one elementary truth, the ignorance of which kills countless ideas and splendid plans, that the moment one definitely commits oneself, then Providence moves too. All sorts of things occur to help one that would never otherwise have occurred. A whole stream of

events issues from the decision, raising in one's favor all manner of unforeseen incidents and meetings and material assistance, which no man could have dreamed would come his way. Whatever you can do, or dream you can, begin it. Boldness has genius, power and magic in it. "

Notice the words, <u>the moment one definitely commits, Providence moves too.</u> You were born to Succeed, but you must take the initiative. Initiative comes first, then you will develop the ability. Most of us want Providence to move before we move.

We want to develop the ability before we commit. We want God to bless us then we will believe. Jesus said, *"You believe, then you will receive. "* (Mark 11:24) If we take people steps, God will take God steps. No wonder most people are unfulfilled, there's a hold-up and no one is moving. Along the lines of commitment, I'm reminded of another verse by the Apostle Paul, when instructing Timothy, in 2 Timothy 2:2, on how to develop leaders:

"And the things you have heard me say in the presence of many witnesses entrust to reliable (committed) men who will develop the ability. "

To live the life we were born to live, we must develop, our commitment, muscles. It can be as simple as making our beds every morning, hanging our clothes every night. Washing the dishes every day, waking up employed each day by planning each day the night before, setting aside time to plan our week and review our goals weekly, exercising three times weekly, etc.

According to Napoleon Hill in his PMA Science of Success Course, "There are six steps which people usually follow in using their mind power for the attainment of their desires. These steps are:

First: The vast majority of people go through life by merely wishing for things. The percentage of people who stop at wishing is estimated to be   70%

Second: A smaller percentage of people develop their wishes into desires. These are estimated to be   10%

Third: A still smaller percentage of the people develop their wishes and desires into hopes. These are estimated to be   8%

Fourth: A still smaller percentage of the people step their mind power up to where it becomes belief. These are estimated to be   6%

Fifth: And yet a very much smaller percentage of the people crystallize their wishes, desires, and hopes into belief, and then into burning desire, and finally faith. This percentage is estimated to be   4%

Sixth: And last a very small percentage of the people take the last two steps, putting their faith into action by planning and acting to carry out their plans. This percentage is estimated to be only   2%

As you can see, committed people, like persistent people, are rare. Persistence and commitment are the twin brothers of achievement in any field. Persistence says I'll do it until; commitment says I'll just do it! Promise yourself to just do it and the rest is history. Committed people always find a way to reach their goals.

The sage of Concord, Ralph Waldo Emerson, put it this way: *"All successful men have agreed in being causationist."*

Hannibal's version goes like this: *"We must either find a way, or make one."*

George B. Shaw put it this way: *"People are always blaming their circumstances for what they are. I don't believe in circumstances, the people who get on in this world are the people who get up and look for the circumstances they want, and if they can't find them, make them."*

You are not a creature of circumstances, chance or environment. Circumstances, chance and environment are largely your own creation, especially if you live in America and are over the age of maturity.

So far we have been building up a lot of firepower, steam and speed, with persistence and commitment. Now is the time to lock on target and attack. In order for us to hit our target, we must have a vision of what we want out of life.

←――――――――――――――――→

Recommended Reading:

It's Always Too Soon to Quit	**Lewis Timberlake**
Stay In The Game	**Crouch**

Vision, Dreams, Goals

"Without a vision the people perish. "

–Proverbs 18:29

Of what use is persistence and commitment if you don't have a vision, dream, desire, or goal you're going for? To have a vision for your life doesn't mean that you predict the future. It simply means that you use your imagination to create a picture of what you will like your future to be.

Vision is that which originates in the mind, based on that which the mind wants to create. You and I are products of God's vision and God's imagination. Remember the words, *"Let us create man in our image. "* Vision, imagination, creativity, dreams and goals are words that will be used interchangeably in this chapter. As usual, this chapter will attempt to challenge you and inspire you to create a vision for yourself. Much has been said and written about goal-setting by a great many people. My suggestion is that you avail yourself of their materials. You will find a list of recommended reading at the end of this chapter.

Napoleon Hill put it this way in P.M.A. Science of Success, "Definiteness of purpose is the starting point of all achievement. Remember this statement . . . *definiteness of purpose is the starting point of all achievement,* and it is the stumbling block of ninety-eight out of every hundred persons because they never really define their goals and start toward them with Definiteness of purpose." Goals are very important.

Habakkuk 2:2-3 reads, *"Write down the revelation and make it plain on tablets so that a herald may run with it. For the revelation awaits an appointed time; it speaks of the end and will not prove false. Though it linger, wait for it; it will certainly come and will not delay."*

That verse is loaded with the concept of goals and persistence.

The Apostle Paul put it this way, *"Brothers, I do not consider myself, yet to have taken hold of it. But one thing I do: forgetting what is behind me and straining toward what is ahead. I press on toward the goal to win the prize for which God has called me heavenward in Christ Jesus."* (Philippians 3:13-14)

If you have failed at goal-setting in the past, forget about it and focus on where you want to go. Whatever you focus on expands.

When Jesus was here on earth, during one of his journeys to Jerusalem, some Pharisees came to Jesus and said to him, *"Leave this place and go somewhere else. Herod wants to kill you."* Jesus replied, *"Go tell that fox, I will drive out demons and heal people today and tomorrow, and the third day, I will reach my goal."* (Luke 13:31-32)

Even Jesus had a goal and was not going to let anyone or anything interfere with his goal!

What are your goals?

Where are you now?

Where are you going?

Answer those questions in reference to your spiritual growth, personal development, health and fitness, finances, family, relationships, etc.

What are your goals? Put them in writing. Do it now! Do it before you go any further. Take a goal-setting break. Goals must be simple, precise, and definite. In setting your goals, let your imagination run free. Put your imagination to work. Make no small plan, dream no small dreams. Vision, imagination, passion, emotion belief, faith, persistence, commitment, focus and enthusiasm must all be put to work when setting your goals. Remember the words of Einstein: *"Imagination is more important than knowledge."*

Shakespeare wrote, *"Imagination makes man a paragon of animals."*

Disraeli said, *"Imagination governs the world."*

George Bernard Shaw wrote, *"Imagination is the beginning of creation. You imagine what you desire; you will what you imagine; and at last you create what you will."*

Henry Ward Beecher in a similar vein said, *"The soul without imagination is what an observatory would be without a telescope."*

Focus your attention on your goals and imagine them fulfilled, and fulfilled they will be with proper attention and persistence over time.

James Allen put it this way, *"Dream lofty dreams, and as you dream, so shall you become. Your vision is the promise of what you shall one day be; your ideal is the prophecy of what you shall at last unveil. The greatest achievement was at first, and for a time, a dream. The oak sleeps in the acorn; the bird waits in the egg; and in the highest vision of the soul, a waking angel stirs. Dreams are the seedlings of realities. Your circumstances may be uncongenial, but they shall not long remain so if you but perceive an ideal and strive to reach it. You cannot travel within and stand still without."*

"Imagination is more important than knowledge."
–Albert Einstein

YOU CAN CHANGE YOUR WORLD BY CONTROLLING YOUR IMAGINATION.

You've probably heard about The Great Stone Face, by Nathaniel Hawthorne. If you haven't, here is your chance. The story goes like this: *On the side of a mountain was The Great Stone Face, which was impressive, strong, kind, honorable. There was a legend that some day a man would appear in town who would look exactly like the face. There also was a young boy who was inspired by the ideals that the face exhibited. So the boy spent his life emulating the face; he would spend hours gazing upon the face on the mountain. He saw great soldiers, merchants, and others come to the town, but none of them resembled the face on the mountain. Until finally one day during a town meeting, he himself was recognized as the Great Stone Face.*

Phenomenal story. We become what we think about. There's an old French proverb that goes like this, *"Be careful what you set your heart on, for you will surely achieve it."*

Keep these facts, quotes and stories in mind as you start planning for your future. Goal-Setting, Dream-Building or whatever you choose to call it is both a science and an art. And that's exactly what we are going to do right now. All through this book I have attempted to present you with several ways to live a Life of Excellence. The next few ideas are by no means the last words on goals, but they are guidelines that will help you become a better goal-setter and goal-getter.

By now you are probably convinced that goal-setting is very important, but I'd like to suggest something that's even more important than goal-setting and that is Mission Clarification. By that I mean the ability to create a vision of the person you would like to become.

You see, mission clarification deals with a complete picture, goal-setting deals with a portion of your mission, and unless your goal is linked to a strong, clear and precise mission,

86

you're probably not going to go full out for your goal, and if you do, you probably will not find total fulfillment. When your goal or desire becomes linked to your mission, it becomes an intention, and intentions are more magnetizing than ordinary goals.

So let's start clarifying your mission by answering the following questions. Please invest some time doing this and write down your answers.

1. **Considering everything, are you happy with your life? I know this is a tough question, but the good news is that you decide what your definition of happiness is. Are you happy with your life? If not, why not? What has to happen in order for you to feel you're happy?**

2. **Where have you been? Where are you now? Where are you going spiritually, mentally, financially, emotionally, socially, physically, and in regards to your family? Come up with the appropriate answers to these questions for the next six months, twelve months, three years, and five years.**

3. **If you continue to think the way you've always thought and you continue to act the way you've always acted, will you reach your goals? If not, what do you need to do differently?**

4. **What do you think your mission in life is? What is your purpose?**

5. **If money was no problem and you had all the time to enjoy all your money, what would you be doing right now? Would you continue working where you are right now? If not, what would you rather be doing?**

6. **If you received a phone call right now, telling you that you just won $5,000,000 (five million dollars), how would that change your life? What would you do with the money? If you don't know, you probably will never receive such a call.**

7. **What would you do differently if you had only six months to live?**

8. What do you really love to do?

9. What have you ever been told you do very well? What have you ever been paid for doing?

10. What do you think you ought to be doing with your life in order for your life to be complete?

11. If it were impossible to fail, what great dreams would you dare to go for?

Review the above questions carefully and then write a statement of what you think your life's purpose is. Take as much time as you need to complete this project. Review your mission statement periodically, until you have one that challenges you to be the best person you can be. Then take the following four steps:

1. Compare your new statement with your current lifestyle. Are they the same? If not, how far apart is your ideal situation from your current reality?

2. Ask yourself what has to happen in order for the two to become one? How much time and effort will this require?

3. Create a plan to bridge the gap. To better help you at this point, I recommend two great tools that I have found to be very helpful in my life. They are, *The Seven Habits Organizer,* by Dr. Stephen Covey, and *Success: The Glen Bland Method,* by Glen Bland.

4. Put your plan into action by investing no less than 30 minutes a day doing something you would be doing if your current reality and ideal situation were the same. Increase this time allotment until your current reality and ideal become one.

Now that you have a mission statement, make a list of your dreams and goals, the things you would like to be doing, and the things you would like to have in life. Here are some ideas to help you. Take time to answer each and every question to your satisfaction:

1. What kind of lifestyle would you want?

2. How much time would you like to invest with your family?

3. How much money would you like to earn monthly?

4. Which charities would you help and give your money to?

5. What kind of home would you live in? Would you be the first family to live in that home? Smell the newness of the carpet!! (smile) Would you have a Jacuzzi? Imagine having a beautiful pool in your back yard, that overlooks the blue lake and the beautiful palm trees in your ideal home.

6. What kind of car would you have parked in your circular driveway?

7. What other goals do you have?

Now turn your dreams into goals by setting a time limit for each one. A goal is a dream with a target date. Now go through your list and decide when you would like to achieve each one of them. Put the time limit next to each goal. For example, if a goal will take you three years to accomplish, write *three* next to it. In selecting your goals keep the following ideas in mind:

1. **Goals should be balanced.**

2. **Goals should be simple and definite.**

3. **Remember the ABC & T of goals.**

    A means **Achievable**

    B means **Believable**

    C means **Controllable**

    T means **Target Date**

4. **Goals should be personal. (Do your homework then come up with your list. Don't let anyone do your thinking for you. What if they are wrong?)**

By now you should have a clearer idea of what you want to do with your life. If you decide to face the next twelve months with these ideas in mind, your life will be more fulfilled. To be sure that the next year is your best ever, we are going to share with you the content of one of my most requested brochures in its entirety (in the following pages). We wrote this brochure several years ago as a means of helping others and ourselves set goals and we have received rave reviews from it. We hope it blesses you as it has many others and us. If you would like to have your own free copy, please write us. (See address in back of this book.)

How To Make This Your Most Prosperous And Productive Year Ever

Ready or not, 12 months from today another year will have come and gone. The question is, will this be just another year? Or will you dare to make it a unique year? Will it be a year that will unleash your ability to design your future and do the things you've wanted to do for a long time?

You can face the next twelve months with fear, aimlessness and anxiety, or you can face them with faith and purpose.

Facing the future with fear and aimlessness leads to frustration, timidity, low self-esteem and probably any other negative emotion you can think of.

On the other hand, facing the future with faith leads to the fulfillment, boldness, courage, achievement and probably any other positive emotion you can think of.

To make the next twelve months your most prosperous and productive year ever, you will need to take the following steps:

Step 1

Choose and decide to make the coming year your best ever. It's that simple because you have the power of choice. You can decide to make today your best day ever by exercising your power of choice. Then make up your mind to stick by that decision every day for the next twelve months. You are probably going to have some not-so-pleasant days; however, if the first thing you do when you arise in the morning is to stick by your decision, you will certainly have many more happy days than you would have had otherwise.

Step 2

Grab a piece of paper or many pieces of paper if you need them. Then at the top of the page, write the following question: What will have to happen in order for the next 12 months to be my most prosperous and productive year ever? Make a list of everything you think will be necessary to make this your best year ever. Here are some ideas to help you.

- How much money would you like to earn?
- How much money would you like to give to worthy causes?
- How many hours would you like to spend developing yourself spiritually, mentally, and emotionally?
- How many books would you like to read monthly?
- How many times a week would you like to exercise?
- How much time would you like to spend with your family?

"Do It Now And Get It Done."
"Seize This Day."

Step 3

Go through your list and decide on your top four goals for the year. Write them on four separate pieces of paper. After each goal, write a statement giving the reasons why you must attain the goal. Make a list of the benefits to be gained and the losses to be avoided by attaining each goal. If you cannot find enough reasons for each goal, then change it and select another goal that will motivate you.

"Without goals people perish."
–Proverbs 29:18

These should be the goals that will make you feel you have had a productive year. You can increase the number of goals if you want. But four seems like a good number to start with.

To make this your most prosperous and productive year ever, you must have a clear picture of what will make it so.

Step 4

You must have a plan. And your plan must include what you can do today to get you one step closer to the attainment of your goal. Your plan does not have to be precise, but it must include what you can do today. A journey of a thousand miles begins with the first step. You are going to live the next 12 months one day at a time. Keep in mind that if your desire to attain the goal is sincere and you continue living by faith, you will certainly reach your goal. The formula for goal attainment is very simple:

- ◆ You must have a goal (your top four goals).
- ◆ You must have a target date (12 months from now).
- ◆ You must have a plan (individual).
- ◆ You must take Action Now!!!

Step 5

Since faith leads to fulfillment, purpose, confidence and achievement, decide to live by faith and not by sight (what you can see, hear, feel, smell, and taste). Faith, simply stated, means *belief without any visible evidence.* You already have faith. All you need to do is develop it by hearing the Word of God and taking appropriate action.

Faith Without Works Is Dead

Step 6

You must develop the habits of success. Yes, habits of success. The only difference between those who make every year their best year ever and those who do not, lies in their habits.

A habit is a pattern of behavior, which can only be acquired by frequent repetition or consistent practice. It usually takes 21-30 days of consistent repetition to form any new habit. According to the late Albert E. N. Gray, in his masterpiece, *The Common Denominator of Success,* he wrote, *"The common denominator of success – the secret of success of every man who has ever been successful – lies in the fact that he formed the habit of doing things that failures don't like to do."* You see the key word is **habit**.

Here is a list of some habits you will need to form in order to make the next twelve months your best ever.

1. Develop the habit of focusing on your goals using words, pictures, and emotions and stay focused.
    ### *FOCUS EQUALS REALITY*

2. Develop the habit of thinking right, speaking right and acting right. The best way to develop these habits is by reading uplifting books and listening to faith-building and inspiring messages consistently.
    ### *THINK, SPEAK, & ACT RIGHT*

3. Develop the habit of planning your work and working your plan.
    ### *PLAN YOUR WORK AND*
    ### *WORK YOUR PLAN*

4. Develop the habit of doing more than you are paid for. Remember, it is more blessed to give than to receive.
    ### *GO THE EXTRA MILE*

5. Develop the habit of doing what you can do today. Make each day count. Your motto should be:
    ### *TNT . . . TODAY NOT TOMORROW*

Step 7

You must stick by the decision you made in Step 1 and make it your purpose until it becomes a **habit**. And then do it for the next twelve months. And remember to, *"Include God in all that you do."* (Acts 17:28; John 15:5)

In order for you and me to make the next twelve months our best ever, we must choose and decide that <u>it will be so</u>. We must live by faith, moved by what we believe, not what we see, hear, or feel. We must have a clear picture of what we want the next twelve months to be like. We must crystallize our thinking by prioritizing our goals. We must have a plan. We must form good habits. We must stick by our decision to form good habits daily until the formation of good habits becomes a habit.

"We must include God in all that we do and get protected if we are not already protected." (Romans 10:9-10)

I dare you to give the next 12 months your best by following these seven steps. If you will give these steps a try, they will give you the success you want, and that you deserve.

Have A Prosperous and Productive New Year

Recommended Reading:

The Magic of Thinking Big **Schwartz**	David
7 Habits of Highly Effective People	Steven Covey
The Instant Millionaire	Mark Fisher
The Power of Positive Thinking	Dr. Peale

Enthusiasm

"Enthusiasm produces the confidence that cries to the world, 'I have what it takes,' without the necessity for your uttering a word."

—Paul J. Meyer

"Nothing great was ever achieved without enthusiasm."

—Ralph Waldo Emerson

Enthusiasm is one of the greatest qualities we need to develop, to fully live a life of excellence. Enthusiasm is not something we need to make up or borrow from somewhere. We already have it, we only need to develop it.

The Webster's new compact *Dictionary* defines enthusiasm as, *ardent eagerness, or zeal.*

Enthusiasm has its origin from two Greek words *En Theos* (God within). The Greeks believe that an enthusiast is a God-intoxicated person, a person with God living inside him driving him onward and upward from victory to victory with unyielding faith. Enthusiasm, like faith, works best when you have a goal or a dream you're going for. Enthusiasm is knowledge on fire. Enthusiasm is faith in action.

"Enthusiasm links knowledge to purpose and gives it driving force."

–Millard Bennett

"Enthusiasm is the twin brother of the will, and is the major source of persistence, sustained action of the will. Will power, persistence, and enthusiasm are triplets which give one sustained action with a minimum loss of physical energy."

–Napoleon Hill

"Enthusiasm moves the world."

–Millard Bennett

"The world belongs to the enthusiast. A man without enthusiasm is like a watch without a mainspring."

–Author Unknown

Orison Swett Marden, one of the pioneers of the personal development movement in the early part of the 20th century described enthusiasm as, *"The great force within us which is perpetually prodding us to do our best . . . an intense feeling of emotion known as a burning desire, without which words fail to carry conviction, deeds fail to impress and actions fall short of their intended mark."*

Enthusiasm is not excitement.

Enthusiasm is real and sincere. It comes from within. It's original, irresistible and permanent.

Excitement is shallow, fake, not convincing and often based on the emotion of the moment.

A good example to illustrate the difference between enthusiasm and excitement is found in the story of the parable of the sower as told by Jesus in the *Bible*. In Mark chapter four, Jesus talks about the seeds that fell along the path, rocky places, among thorns and on the good ground. Only the seed that fell on the good ground produced the thirty, sixty, and the hundred-fold return.

Excitement is like the first three groups of seeds that have an appearance of success, but deep inside are shallow.

Enthusiasm is like the seed that fell on the good soil, which produced the thirty, sixty, and hundred fold return. A man with enthusiasm is a majority, because wherever he turns he is able to persuade others to his way of thinking. Perhaps it's that knowledge that prompted Henry Chester to write his superb dissertation on enthusiasm. He wrote:

"Enthusiasm is one of the greatest assets of man. It beats money and power and influence. Single-handed the enthusiast convinces and dominates where the wealth accumulated by a small army of workers would scarcely raise a tremor of interest. Enthusiasm tramples over prejudice and opposition, spurns inaction, storms the citadel of its object and like an avalanche overwhelms and engulfs all obstacles.

"It is nothing less than faith in action. Faith and initiative rightly combined remove mountainous barriers and achieve the unheard of and miraculous. Set the germ of enthusiasm afloat in your plant, your office or on your farm. Carry it in your attitude and manner. It will spread and influence every fiber of your industry before you realize it. It will mean increase in production and decrease in cost; joy, pleasure, and satisfaction to your workers; life-real and virile; spontaneous, rock-bed results; the vital things that pay big dividends throughout your life."

Coming back to my story again, an enthusiast is like that seed, which fell on good soil and produced the thirty, sixty, and hundred fold return, mowing down all opposition, bad weather, thorns, thistles and every other obstacle.

In our situation, an enthusiast is that person who goes for his dream, mowing down all doubts, fears, worries, handicaps and every other obstacle imaginable.

Enthusiasm is the ability to transfer that which you feel and believe to another person in the same spirit of faith that you feel and believe, so that the other person accepts your ideas.

Enthusiasm is not a gimmick to be used to take advantage of others. As a matter of fact, a man without real enthusiasm is like a carbonated drink without carbon dioxide or like a crab cake without the crabmeat; it just doesn't fit. A **true** enthusiast is always sincere.

How To Develop the Habit of Enthusiasm

You can develop the habit of enthusiasm by doing the following:

1. Find out what you really love to do, then do it.

2. Find out what benefits you will gain by doing it.

3. Bombard your mind by conditioning yourself with as much information as you can about your subject matter, using words, pictures, and emotions. Make sure this is information that inspires you.

4. Visualize yourself doing what you love to do and enjoy it.

5. Do something that will move you closer to your goal every day and on a consistent basis and never give up until you reach your goal.

6. Associate with people you consider to be enthusiastic.

7. Act enthusiastically by walking, talking, and smiling with a spirit

of fervor and zest.

It takes courage to be enthusiastic, especially in a world where we have more fire fighters than fire. Just in case you don't know who fire fighters are, they are the people who are ready to water down any good idea you have. They know why things wouldn't work even though they've never accomplished anything in their lives. Closely related to fire fighters are alligators. They are the people, who like alligators, have very big mouths but brains the size of a lima bean. Have the courage to cut yourself away from these people.

It takes courage to be enthusiastic, to live a life of excellence, but you know enough by now to realize that you will need to persevere. And if you get into a tight place when everything seems to go against you, remember the words of Emerson who wrote:

"Whatever you do, you need courage. Whatever course you decide upon, there is always someone to tell you that you're wrong, there are always difficulties arising which tempt you to believe your critics are right, to map out a course of action and follow it to the end requires some of the same courage which a soldier needs. Peace has its victories, but it takes brave men to win them. Make the most of yourself for that is all there is of you."

← ————————————————— →

Recommended Reading:

Life Is Tremendous	Charles "T" Jones
The Greatest Salesman In the World	Og Mandino
See You At the Top	Zig Ziglar
Enthusiasm Makes the Difference	Dr. Peale

Work

"All hard work brings a profit, but mere talk leads only to poverty."

—Proverbs 14:23

"Genius is one percent inspiration, and ninety-nine percent perspiration."

—Thomas Edison

Up until now we've been talking about the fact that we were born to Succeed. We've also talked about several universal laws as well as the factors, which affect how our minds and brains work. We've talked about some of the qualities necessary to live a life of Excellence, but these ideas alone will not move us an inch from where we are, unless we put these ideas to work.

Work is one of the greatest joys of life, but unfortunately most people in our society have come to see work as an unnecessary evil that is imposed upon us against our will. Nothing could be farther from the truth. To the right-thinking person, work is both a privilege and a joy, which helps us become all that we were created to be.

Work as we are referring to here is not limited to physical work only. In order for us to live lives of Excellence, we must continue to work on developing ourselves spiritually, mentally, emotionally, and physically. We must continue to work on our relationships to improve them. We must continue to improve our skills.

According to the *Bible,* in the book of Genesis, when God created man, He commanded man to be fruitful, increase in number and have dominion over all of creation. It takes work of some kind to be fruitful and increase in number. Later on God put man in the Garden of Eden to work it and take care of it. From this brief account we can see that the Creator's intention for His creation (man) was not for him to be idle but to work. Later on, God gave man a promotion by bringing all the animals to man, so man could name them (creative work).

God, who created man to grow and multiply, deposited a lot of gifts, talents and abilities in man that can only be fully developed by working. Work alone is the miracle ingredient that helps us become all that we were meant to be. But unfortunately many of us resent work. We fail to realize that opportunity, fame, fortune, and fulfillment often disguise themselves as hard work.

The great writer and philosopher Henry David Thoreau once wrote that, *"Most people lead lives of quiet desperation."* Work, when approached with the right mental attitude, will cure all desperation and depression known to man. Most of the psychosomatic diseases that people have are the result of not doing all they can do. Low self-esteem, lack of ambition, depression, worry, stress, and poverty are mostly a result of laziness. Lest I be misunderstood, I am not suggesting that hard work alone will make anyone rich, famous or successful. Because I know better. I am however suggesting that no matter what else we do, if we don't work, we will not get desirable results. The Apostle Paul wrote to the Thessalonians, *"If a man will not work, he shall not eat."* (2 Thessalonians 3:10)

Ralph Waldo Emerson wrote in his essay titled *Compensation*:

"Do the thing and you shall have the power," and Proverbs 10:4 reads, *"Lazy hands make a man poor, but diligent hands bring wealth."*

Every great and successful person who has ever lived and who is living today has achieved greatness by working for it. Even God Himself worked for six days before he rested, and He commanded us to do the same. However, these days people are always trying to get away with doing less and less. I'm sure some people would love the idea of working one day and relaxing six days. Jim Michaels once said, *"Too many workers would rather get home than get ahead."* And I once heard of a medical doctor who said that most heart attacks occur on Monday mornings at 9:00 a.m. That's probably because the thought of work terrifies them.

Whatever we do we should do it with a pleasant attitude, since we now have enough information as a result of reading this book to change our lives. We should view our work as stepping stones.

Because we were born to work and to do creative exploits, nature severely discourages idleness and emptiness. It is only the act of working by using our body and mind that helps us become co-creators of our lives with God and nature.

Dr. Myles Monroe put the importance of work brilliantly in his book, *Releasing Your Potential,* this way:

"Work always produces more personal growth and satisfaction than rest does. It stirs up your creative abilities and draws from the hidden store of your potential. If you are unfulfilled, you're probably resting too much. You're getting bored because you aren't working. You can't run from work and expect to be happy. Work is the energy that keeps you alive. It's the stuff that gives life meaning. Having six weeks of vacation is not the supreme measure of success or the ultimate prescription for happiness."

To realize our full potential, to fulfill our desires, to be fruitful and multiply, to lead a life of Excellence, we must work. Work is one of those things in life that is not an option, but a must. Everywhere you see a successful person or enterprise, for the most part, you see a product of lots of work and effort. Most people want more money, fame, success, and the like, but do not realize that in order to get more and become more, what they have must be maximized.

"A man reaps what he sows."

–Galatians 6:7

In order for our work to help us realize our full potential, we should seek the kind of work that has, but is not limited to, the following characteristics:

1. Our work must be a challenge. It's the challenge that helps us realize how much we can do and it's the challenge that helps us fulfill ourselves, and realize our potential by making the most of our skills, talents, and abilities.

2. Our work must be meaningful. When we see where our work, no matter how small it is, fits into a larger scope, we become motivated to give it our all.

3. Our work must be fulfilling. We must feel a sense of fulfillment in order for us to want to do all we can do. Our work must contribute to other people's lives. We must feel that we are helping others solve their problems in life. A Pastor feels fulfilled because he realizes he is leading people to their Creator. A doctor feels good because he is helping people solve their health problems.

"The longer I live the more I am convinced that the one thing worth living for and dying for is the privilege of making someone more happy and more useful. No man who ever does anything to lift up his fellows ever makes a sacrifice."

–Booker T. Washington

4. Our work must provide us with financial rewards. As a matter of fact, this appears to be the most important reason why people work. If your work does not provide you with all the money you need to support your lifestyle, you might want to consider rendering more service, you might want to consider starting your own home-based or part-time business.

Recommended Reading:

The Richest Man in Babylon	**George Clason**
Motivational Classics	**Charles T. Jones**
University of Success	**Og Mandino**

Enhanced Health And Vitality
The Five Essentials To Wellness

"A sound mind in a sound body: is a short, but full description of a happy state in this world."
                                                    –John Locke

God created us as a whole being, therefore He is interested in us as a whole person. He wants us to grow near to Him spiritually, He wants our minds to be sound and our bodies to be healthy.

"Beloved I wish above all things that you prosper and be in good health, even as your soul prospers." (John 3:2)

Our body is the house or vehicle in which we live to help us fulfill our destiny on the earth. It is a very strong, yet delicate machinery that needs proper care for it to maximize its full potential. Just like your vehicle (car) comes with a proper care and maintenance guide, there is proper care and maintenance for your vehicle called "body." We believe the five essentials to health and vitality need to be addressed in order to live a good and abundant life.

Up to this point we have been talking about the qualities of excellence. All these qualities however will do us no good unless we have an abundance of health and vitality. The five essentials to wellness are by no means the last words on health, but they will provide you with principles for improving the quality of your life, health and over all vitality. In this chapter you will discover the essentials of what's good for your body, what's good for your mind, and the connection the mind has with the body. You can use this information to begin to breakthrough to greater heights of success, vitality, peace of mind and ultimately live your life to its fullest potential.

Essential #1 – Goals For Your Health

Goals are essential to achievement as we have seen in a previous chapter. The same concepts that were discussed earlier also apply to your health and well-being. We need to have specific goals in terms of our health and vitality in order to achieve them.

For example:

1. How much would you like to weigh?

2. How many times a week would you like to exercise?

3. What would you like your cholesterol count to be?

4. How active and vitally alive would you like to be?

You need to write your goals down. There is something magical about writing goals. It seems as if God causes the whole universe to come together and move on your behalf to make your goals a reality. Remember to be very specific with your goals.

Your health is the greatest wealth you have. And without it, all else is meaningless. So come up with a plan of exactly what you want to achieve, and then back your plan up with action.

Track your goals. Make necessary adjustments weekly, monthly, quarterly, or as needed. Once you've done these things you would have begun your journey towards increased health and vitality.

Essential #2 – Right Thinking and Sound Mind

"Disease and health, like circumstances are rooted in thought. Sickly thoughts express themselves through a sickly body. Thoughts of fear have been known to kill as quickly as a bullet . . . People who live in fear of disease are the same people who get it."

–James Allen

There is a new discipline that proclaims the mind and body connection and it is called psycho-neuro-immunology. Your mind has a direct communication system to your body and immune system. God made your mind so powerful, that depending on your state of mind, what you picture in your imagination, and what you say to yourself (self-talk), can keep you well or make you sick.

We all have from time to time experienced the emotions of stress, tension, worry, anxiety and fear. Unfortunately, these negative emotions can lead to negative responses in our immune system, causing our defenses to shut down. When our defenses are shut down our body becomes prey for all kinds of illnesses and diseases. It usually does not happen immediately, but over a period of time it can be devastating. These negative emotions all have their roots in fear. Your soul (your mind, will, and emotions) attracts to itself the things it loves and the things it fears.

"For the thing I greatly feared has come upon me, and what I dreaded has happened to me."

–Job 3:25

Medical experts have said that 75% of all doctor visits, for various ailments have their root in the emotional disorders of stress, anxiety and worry. In our endeavor to live a life of health and vitality we must cultivate our thoughts on a daily basis. **We must think on the things we want to happen, and not let our minds dwell on what we do not want.**

When we think good and happy thoughts toward people, things and situations, and when we read good books, listen to good tapes, set and achieve our goals, we release a chemical in our body called endorphins. Endorphins are healing or "feel good" agents that are released into our bodies through positive thoughts, and exercise. They give us a natural high and help to ward off sickness and disease.

"A happy heart (or mind) is like a good medicine"
(Proverbs 17:22)

If you want to protect your body and its health, protect your mind.

"Don't ever forget my words. Keep them always in your mind; they are the key to life to those who find them and they bring health to the whole body. Be careful what you think because your thoughts run your life."
(Proverbs 4:21-23)

"Strong, pure, happy thoughts build the body in vigor and grace."
–James Allen

Since the body tends to obey the mind, take time to meditate on (or put in your mind) things that will give the body its fullness of vitality.

The *Bible* gives us instruction on the things we should think on.

> *"Finally Brethren, whatever things are true, whatever things are noble, whatever things are lovely, whatever things are of good report, if there is any virtue and if there is anything praiseworthy, meditate and think on these things.*
>
> *–Philippians 4:8*

Meditate on thoughts of love, joy, peace, goodness, kindness, gentleness, patience, faithfulness, and self-control. Whenever a thought comes into your mind that you don't want, cast it out immediately, and then replace it with a good thought. As you have learned earlier in this book, when you practice this enough times you will find a new habit being formed, and your thoughts will become more and more positive. Positive thoughts have a direct correlation with a healthy body.

> *"Change of diet will not help you unless you change your thoughts. Purify your thoughts, and you will no longer desire impure food."*
>
> *–James Allen*

Essential #3 – Right Eating and Proper Nutrition

What we eat is as important as what we think when it comes to our health and vitality. Natural foods such as raw fruits, vegetables, salads, nuts, sprouts, and green leaf vegetables (such as spinach, broccoli, turnips, collards, kale, etc.) help our bodies fight and ward off diseases, impurities, and sicknesses. When foods are uncooked, they maintain vital life enzymes. Enzymes are the LIFE in our foods and they nourish the LIFE in our body which are our cells. When we intake meat (processed food, full of fat and cholesterol), cooked foods, and junk foods, we are eating foods that give very little nourishment to our body and, in particular, to our cells. When cells are not properly nourished they get sickly and die. Eventually these bad cells manifest themselves through a sickly body and consume lots of energy from us.

Here are a few suggestions for proper nutrition and right eating.

1. Eat water-rich foods since the human body is about 70% water.

At least 70% of our diet should consist of water-rich foods such as salads, vegetables, and fruits. Drinking extracted raw vegetable and fruit juices helps to re-build and regenerate our cells and tissues. These water-rich foods and juices can serve as medicine if consumed in their natural state. If we do not eat and drink the right kinds of foods, which nourish the body constructively, the body can waste away into suffering and eventually premature death. So go out today and buy a juicer (**The Champion** brand, is a very good one) and try to eat a fresh salad at least once a day. Drink lots of water (8 glasses or more daily) and experience health and vitality to the highest degree.

2. Optimize your energy level with proper food combinations

> a) Don't eat proteins and carbohydrates together (such as: meat and potatoes, or spaghetti with meat sauce).
>
> b) Eat a vegetable with any protein (meat) or carbohydrate (starch).
>
> c) Don't drink liquids with meals. Instead drink your liquids approximately 30 minutes before or wait 30 minutes after the meal so your body can experience maximum digestion for energy.

3. **Eat heavy food only between the hours of 12 noon and 8 p.m. to better maximize your energy.**

4. **Eat Fruit Correctly**

   a) Don't eat melons with any other fruit.

   b) Don't mix fruit with other foods.

   c) Sweet fruit (such as bananas) should be eaten after other fruits.

   d) Fruits should be eaten preferably before 12:00 noon to assist in the elimination process.

5. **Fast Your Way To Increased Health**

Fasting is nature's way of house cleaning. By abstaining from foods for a pre-determined period of time, our body is forced to feed upon its own morbid waste, toxins, and poisons that are stored up in the tissues and cells because there is no food to feed upon. This process eventually expels the toxins right out of the body.

Here are some suggestions:

1. **Try fasting one day per week to start with, drinking only water for 24 hours. By doing this you will have fasted for 52 days out of the year. Wow, what an opportunity for cleansing.**

2. **Get a copy of the *Miracle of Fasting* by Paul and Patricia Bragg and devour the information.**

Essential #4 – Exercise and Movement

Our bodies were designed to have lots of physical activity. Our bodies are composed of tissue cells that require daily stimulation to maintain elasticity and pliability. You know the old saying, "Use or you lose it."

If cells are not exercised they cease to function. If they are not functioning then they cannot produce healthy new cells.

These dead cells soon become accumulated waste in the tissues of the body. The lymph system (the body's protectant which works with your immune system) if not exercised, will not be able to fight off and cleanse the body of waste because the fluid remains stagnant. Muscles begin to atrophy without exercise. The heart muscle in particular needs exercise to keep the risk of clogged arteries, heart attack, and strokes down.

Exercising improves circulation, improves mental function, releases endorphins (healing agents), lowers depression and anxiety, keeps muscles elastic and strong, and flushes toxins from the tissues of the body.

Here is a suggestion: Health and Fitness experts recommend exercising for 20-45 minutes at least 3-5 times a week. Walking seems to be the most ideal form of exercise.

Essential # 5 – Rest and Relaxation

Even though physical activity is great, the body needs a balance. The body needs sufficient rest, relaxation (mind and body), and sleep. The purpose of relaxation and sleep is again so that the body can cleanse and restore itself. This is the time to repair and build its cells.

Have you noticed, all throughout this chapter that the body does a lot to protect its cells? Cells are the life force. The body everyday is always moving toward health and vitality. When people get sick, they have worked overtime to make that happen, because the body is constantly fighting for health. There is nothing from the outside that can cure you. The key to great health is to remove the obstacles (such as toxins, and negative thoughts) that stand in the way of the body healing itself.

Here are some suggestions:

- Get adequate rest (6-8 hours of sleep daily).

- Take daily naps (30 minutes to one hour).

- Take time daily to dream and think on good things.

- Take several two to five day vacations this year to relax (see pages 143 & 144).

- Learn to enjoy nature and appreciate this great world God has given us.

- Set aside time with family and friends and have a time of laughter and fun.

In Conclusion:

God created everything in abundance. Therefore, I believe God has given us everything we need in this life to have an abundance of health and high vitality. Health is our Birthright. If we will just flow with nature and not against her, keeping our thoughts pure, eating right, and exercising, we'll find ourselves feeling better and living longer.

Part IV

Human Engineering

So far we have covered some of the reasons why we must dare to excel in life as well as some qualities that we need to develop. The next few pages, however, are probably even more important than all we've covered so far. I say this for the simple reason that this topic is the warp and the woof of all success. Just in case you are still wondering what this is about, I'm making reference to harmonious human relations. Let's face it, almost everything worthwhile that you and I are ever going to do will involve people. It therefore makes a lot of sense to cover some of the qualities that make for successful human relationships. Unfortunately, this is the one section of this book I feel least qualified to write about because I still have a long way to go myself. Fortunately, you and I now know a little bit more about how the brain works to be able to handle this topic if we are sincere enough.

Here are some ideas that are guaranteed to enhance the quality of all your relationships if you apply them.

Forgiveness

Forgiveness is a term that most of us take lightly. However, if we fully understand the impact it can have on the quality of our lives, and if we then develop the habit of forgiving on a consistent basis, we will be well on our way to leading a peaceful, harmonious and serene life. To forgive means to give something for. It means to cancel a debt or trespass or a wrong done. Most of us have a tendency to use the word forgiveness lightly. Forgiveness is both a natural and spiritual law. When we hurt ourselves physically, for example in the case of a cut on our body, nature forgives us by healing the wound over a period of time, in most cases in as little as a few weeks.

When we hurt ourselves emotionally or spiritually due to our disobedience of God's law, He forgives us, if we sincerely ask Him. But unfortunately, most of us have a tough time forgiving ourselves much less others and this is probably the cause of most of the problems we have in dealing with people. We are very fragile and sensitive creatures. We are created with a tremendous capacity to love and be loved, but unfortunately we use that capacity to hurt ourselves and others.

Anger, resentment, envy, cynicism, revenge, jealousy, fear, suspicion, superstition, intolerance, and unforgiveness are some of the emotions that prevent us from reaching our potential. Most of us will be more happy and successful in life if all we do is get rid of these disempowering emotions. What we all need, to be more successful in life and to live a life of Excellence, is not more money, or opportunity, or more knowledge, but more love. More love for God, more love for our fellow men and women, more love for ourselves, and more love for all created things. The Apostle John put it well when he penned these immortal words, *"Perfect love casts out all fear."* (John 4:18)

The true test of forgiveness can be judged by how you react to a person or an event you felt wronged by in the past. For example: If someone hurt you a few years ago and you claim to have forgiven the person, and you still get agitated when you hear the person's name mentioned, then that is proof you have not completely forgiven. Do you remember the example of the cut on the body we used earlier? If you suffered a cut a few years ago and nature has forgiven you by healing you, you still have memories of the cut but it will not upset you. Once we have truly forgiven a person or event, we should be able to meet that person in our thoughts or in person just like water meets water, with no anger, or resentment left in us.

Here are two critical reasons why we need to forgive others immediately:

1. Unforgiveness is nothing but an excess emotional baggage that hurts us more than the person we have something against. Unforgiveness involves passing judgment on others. Perhaps that's why Jesus admonished us, *"Do not judge, or you too will be judged. For in the same way you judge you will be judged, and with the measure you use it will be measured to you. "* (Matthew 7:1-2)

2. When we refuse to forgive we pass judgment against others, and guess where the judgment is taking place? It is in our hearts and minds. This means we are simply passing judgment on ourselves, since we become what we think about. The person we are passing judgment against probably has no idea what is going on with us. When we refuse to forgive others, that *unforgiveness* takes root in our hearts.

We already know that what we feel we attract and what we imagine we become. So guess who gets hurt when we refuse to forgive? We do. So muster up all the courage you can and develop the habit of forgiving others. *"For if you forgive men when they sin against you, your heavenly Father will also forgive you. "* (Matthew 6:14)

Forgiveness creates an opening for us to experience abundance, peace, harmony and goodwill of all kinds, for the simple reason that when we forgive we let go of the excess baggage we don't need to be carrying anyway. Forgiveness makes it easy for us to think straight, right and positively. Unforgiveness is like the clog that prevents water from flowing freely in your faucet. Forgiveness is like the chemical or tool that removes the clog and lets you experience the free flow.

Unforgiveness is like the excess fat and cholesterol that clogs the arteries. It sometimes costs people their lives. Forgiveness is like the miraculous procedure that cleans the arteries and gives some a new lease on life. Unforgiveness is spiritual, mental, emotional and physical death. Forgiveness is life in all ways and along all lines.

LOVE

What is love? That's a good question to which I don't fully know the answer, for the simple reason that everything I will attempt to say here is an attempt to describe love. Love is greater than the sum of its parts. However, if you want a Biblical and simple definition of love, I would have to say God is love. Let's get back to our subject on how to develop harmonious human relationships. I thought it would be better to approach this question at its source as opposed to trying to come up with strategies that just make us appear to be genuinely interested in getting along well with others.

In this section I'm going to attempt to give you the many definitions of love I have come across. I'm going to interpret some of them and leave the rest to you. The important thing for us to remember is that love, like forgiveness, has to do with giving. Love is not just a sentimental emotion or feeling. Love is an act. Love simply put means going the extra mile. Love is an outward expression of our internal spiritual nature.

Love is the mainspring of life.

Love is the panacea (cure-all) of all man's illnesses.

Love is the "Elan vital" (the life giving force).

Love is the eternal Elixir (the everlasting life-prolonger).

As the Apostle Paul put in First Corinthians, chapter 13:4-8:

> "Love is patient,
> "Love is kind,
> "Love does not envy,
> "Love does not boast,
> "Love is not proud,

"Love is not rude,
"Love is not self seeking,
"Love is not easily angered,
"Love keeps no record of wrongs,
"Love does not delight in evil but rejoices with the truth,
"Love always protects,
"Love always trusts,
"Love always hope,
"Love always perseveres,
"Love never fails. "

How do you like these definitions for starters? Better yet, how do you compare? As I mentioned earlier, I really cannot tell you what love is except what the *Bible* says. However, I can assure you that love is a quality we can all develop if we are sincere about wanting to get along with other people. It is my belief that we as people created in God's image, all have the seed of God's love deposited in us. All we need to do is to fan the flame of that love and develop this quality that alone can make us as successful and happy as we care to be.

How To Develop More Love

1. The first step to developing this quality is to become very familiar with the definition of love as described by the Apostle Paul.

2. Next, since you have the seed of God's love in you; replace your name everywhere you see the word *Love* in Apostle Paul's definition. Knowing what you know about conditioning and also realizing that like attracts like and that a man reaps what he sows, you know that by meditating on the qualities of love, sooner or later you will start demonstrating them in your life if you are sincere and persistent enough.

3. Control your thoughts, words and actions toward others. Be very slow to judge, condemn or criticize and be very quick to praise and look for the good in others. Remember whatever you think, say or do to another, you think, say, or do to yourself.

4. Fill your mind with thoughts of love as much as you can. Pray to God to help you become more sincerely and genuinely loving towards others, and really mean it. Remember we are not talking about a way to manipulate others, but we are talking about ideas and concepts that will help us develop the wonderful qualities that reside within us. At this point I would like to share with you a simple prayer that I pray to keep my mind focused on God's love for the benefit of others. Whenever I start feeling agitated, frustrated, and uncomfortable, I quietly repeat the following prayer over and over again until I become poised, serene, confident and calm. Here it is :

"God's love fills my heart and I radiate love, peace, prosperity and good will to all."

I also use this prayer whenever I am communicating with people whom I am currently on very good terms with so as to make the good even better. For example, when I am about to speak to my wife, I would pray like this:

"God's love fills my heart and I radiate love, peace, prosperity, and good will to Denise."

This prayer works for me, so you can feel free to borrow it if you want. I promise not to charge you any interest.

Lest you forget, we are still talking about how to develop harmonious human relationships. Similarly, the same steps used in developing love can be used to develop the habit of forgiveness. At this point I would like to emphasize the fact that loving someone does not mean you associate with that person. It simply means you wish them well. It means you have no malice towards others. Better yet, it means that as much as it depends on you, you will promote their success. This is not really difficult to do since you and I probably have a lot of politicians, athletes and movie stars we think we love without necessarily associating with them. Some of them don't even know we exist. The reason we can do that is because true love is of the heart.

All that we've covered up till now, is the foundation upon which to develop harmonious human relationships. By the time you master the art and science of forgiving and loving people, you will have attained a degree as Doctor of Human Engineering. Love and forgiveness are two loaded words that some of us will never fully understand except for the grace and mercy of God. The next section is going to focus on some specific qualities that can make the above accomplishment even better.

How To Develop An Excelling Personality

Personality is the sum total of one's spiritual, mental, emotional and physical characteristics that distinguish one person from another. An Excelling personality is that personality that enables one to Excel in whatever his or her calling. Since our personality represents the totality of who we are, it behooves us to now analyze some of the factors that make for an Excelling Personality.

1. **Optimism:** Optimism includes primarily what goes on in your heart, mind and head. It involves the way you think towards and about other people. It involves your goals, hopes, aspirations and your faith in God, other people and yourself. It involves your courage, your ability to take risks. Others easily pick up all of these factors, which in turn makes others become attractive to you. A pessimist is seldom found with many worthwhile goal-oriented people. And an optimist is never wanting for wholesome life-enhancing relationships.

2. **Empathy:** To develop an excelling personality in this world filled with different philosophies, ideas and opinions, one needs to be empathetic toward the views, opinions, beliefs, etc., of others. Empathy means that you understand how the other person feels but you do not feel that way yourself. It means to be flexible enough to realize that other people might have more information than we do on certain subjects. It means the willingness and desire to understand other people. Empathy is the ability to adapt to different situations without choking under pressure.

3. **Sincerity:** Sincerity with oneself is the first step in being sincere with others. And without a sincere genuine interest in others'

welfare, no one can truly develop that personality that excels. We need to be sincere in our motives, in terms of what we think, speak and do. An insincere person cannot go too far before being discovered, because insincerity writes itself indelibly into one's thoughts, acts and deeds. Shakespeare put it well when he wrote:

"To thine own self be true, and it must follow as the night the day. Thou canst not then be false to any man."

4. **Decisiveness:** The person who can make decisions promptly and stand by them is bound to be a leader among his or her peers. The essence of an excelling personality is leadership and leadership involves making decisions when all necessary facts are available. A decisive leader who tempers his decisions with love and forgiveness is bound to attract dependable and loyal associates.

5. **Courtesy and Politeness:** If love and forgiveness are the heart of developing harmonious human relationships, courtesy and politeness are the hands and feet. Courtesy and politeness involve going the extra mile in the little things that mean a lot. It involves respecting the rights and feelings of other people regardless of their position in life and particularly towards those people who are in a different position than we are. It involves saying thank you, recognizing the presence of others, respecting all people, giving a smile to brighten someone else's day, giving a hand to lighten someone's load, giving the other driver the right of way and so on.

6. **Common Sense:** Tact and skill. Someone has said common sense is so common that it is no longer common. Common sense and tact involve doing and saying the right thing at the right time. To develop an excelling personality, one needs to develop certain crucial skills, some of which includes the appropriate use of words (vocabulary). One also needs to master the skill of voice modulation. Sometimes it's not what we say that matters, but how we say it.

"Clothe yourselves with compassion, kindness, humility, gentleness, and patience." (Colossians 3:12)

7. **Personal Appearance:** Personal appearance involves not only what we wear physically, but it also involves our spiritual and mental appearance. To develop an excelling personality, we need to clothe our insides with appropriate attitudes, compassion and humility. We need to clothe our bodies with appropriate apparels, and most importantly, we should wear a smile as much as possible. We need to pay special attention to our facial expressions. Our facial expressions, especially our smile, are what others see first.

To be appropriately clothed inside and outside is the secret to becoming an attractive person. Let us not forget the importance of a firm handshake in developing an excelling personality. Once our facial expressions have attracted others, the two other ways of communicating with others are through our voices and handshakes.

8. **Tolerance:** Tolerance is closely related to empathy and flexibility because this quality allows us to become all things to all people, so long as we don't compromise our personal beliefs. Tolerance allows us to live and let others live. Tolerance makes us realize that most people around us do whatever they do because that's the best they can do considering their situation. Tolerance does not mean we allow people to make excuses, but it allows us to walk in another's moccasins for a mile before making a comment.

9. **Emotional Mastery:** To become attractive to others and to develop an excelling personality, we need to become masters of our emotions. Our emotions can easily run out of control if we don't learn to discipline ourselves. The motto of the true leader should be: **Think before you speak so that you will not regret what you say. Be slow to speak and quick to listen and forgive.**

In addition to mastering these nine factors of developing an excelling personality, do all you can to eliminate the scratchy elements out of your personality. Remember: **If it is to be it's up to you. Much success to you!**

Recommended Reading

How To Win Friends and Influence People	Dale Carnegie
The Greatest Thing in the World	Henry Drummond
The Power of Your Subconscious Mind	Dr. Joseph Murphy
Skill With People	Les Giblin

PART V

My Own Story

This portion of the book is dedicated to you, the serious, committed, and persistent leader. Success is your birthright, and this is your opportunity to write your own success story. Much success to you.

Additional Information

For additional information about The Life Enrichment Institute and other Life Enriching programs, seminars and services send a self-addressed stamped envelope to:

The Life Enrichment Institute
P. O. Box 529
Burtonsville, MD 20866
(301) 890-3405

To receive a special gift bonus, visit us at out Web Site:

www.bookworld.com/success

Discover the Secret of

Increasing Your Mental Ability in 90 Days or Less With our READ AND GROW RICH winners program

Did you know that the average person reads less than one book a year? If you would like to get on a reading program that would <u>revolutionize</u> and <u>transform</u> your life for the better, order our Read and Grow Rich Winner's Pack which includes:

1) A list of books that will <u>enrich your Life in all ways</u> and along all lines.

2) A 90-day reading program that is guaranteed to reenergize every fiber and cell of your being.

3) A special report titled **"What every serious leader needs to know about reading."**

To receive your **special package,** send a check or money order for $9.95 to

Life Enrichment Institute
P.O. Box 529
Burtonsville, MD 20866
or call 301-890-3405

Empower Your Life With
Life Enriching Seminars
Keynote speeches and seminars!

Here are four of the outstanding seminars and workshops offered by the Life Enrichment Institute featuring Larry and Denise Adebesin and other outstanding speakers.

Success: It's Your Birthright

If you are interested in co-creating your destiny and living the lifestyle of your dreams, this seminar is for you. Every participant will receive a workbook as well as a PERSONALIZED MISSION CLARIFICATION MANUAL to help chart your course to the destiny of your choice. Choose to attend this seminar and change your life for the better FOREVER.

Living Beyond Limits (Seminar: Health & Vitality)

"Health is not just the absence of a disease, it's a joyfulness that should be inside us all the time. It's a state of positive well being which is <u>physical</u>, <u>emotional</u>, <u>psychological</u>, and <u>spiritual</u>." This seminar will show you how to overcome your limiting beliefs, fears, and doubts. You will learn what's good for the mind, what's good for the body and the connection they have to one another. And you will learn how to live life abundantly.

Sell Your Way To The Top

"Persistent people begin their success where others end in failure." This seminar is designed to help develop sales qualities that causes you to be extraordinary in the marketplace. Your income will seldom exceed your personal development. So this seminar focuses on developing attitudes, states of mind, characteristics, and fundamental principles that can skyrocket your income when applied. This is not your usual sales course. This is a course about getting results.

Ordinary People Creating Extraordinary Abundance (Seminar & Workshop)

"Money is of the pocket, wealth is a state of mind." In this seminar you will learn how to overcome your limiting beliefs about abundance and prosperity. You will also learn how to immediately and easily create that state of mind that allows you to attract abundance and manifest prosperity in your life. You will learn the fundamentals of financial planning, investing and how to simplify and grow rich. This seminar will give you peace of mind regarding your finances like you've never experienced. You will also receive your Personalized Financial Plan that will show you how to reach your ultimate financial goals.

Call Larry or Denise Adebesin at 301-890-3405 to schedule your next conference or to find out about upcoming Life Enriching Seminars.

Special Offers

Personal Enrichment Tapes

"Renewing the Mind Series"

According to a George Washington University Survey, bad news is recorded on TV 20% more then good news. The average person hears the word "no" or "you can't do it" about 148,000 times by the time he or she reaches age 18.

Our minds are so bombarded with negativity that we become full of fear, worry, stress, and then the future becomes bleak. It is no wonder why people roam aimlessly throughout life, with unfulfilled dreams, unfulfilled hopes, and settling for a life of mediocrity.

Now here is your opportunity to get on top, and take immediate control of your destiny by RENEWING YOUR MIND. These tapes are designed to enhance the whole person (spirit, soul, and body). When you renew your mind positively, you can begin to attract the things you want out of life, instead of what you do not want. Become the person you've always wanted to be. Order the Personal Enrichment Tapes today and see your life change forever.

RM1 *Wealth: It's Your Birthright*

RM2 *Health & Vitality: It's Your Birthright*

RM3 *Believing in Yourself*

RM4 *Overcoming Fear & Panic*

RM5 *Peace of Mind: It's Your Birthright*

RM6 *Reducing Stress & Anxiety*

RM7 *Discovering Your Hidden Treasures*

Regular: $9.95 . . . *Special* *Offer* . . . Buy Three and Get One FREE

Order Form

Quantity	Description	Unit Price	Total Cost

Subtotal	_____
Taxes (MD residents 5%)	_____
Shipping $2.00 plus $1.00 for each additional item	_____
Total	_____

Special Offers

"Success It's Your Birthright Tapes"

Yes Larry and Denise, I want to take advantage of the following great offer:

(#1) _____Yes, I want to take advantage of your 60 day 100% absolute money back guarantee. Enclosed is my check for $12.95 for *Success: It's Your Birthright* (the book).

(#2) "Success: It's Your Birthright" on Tape
Discover how this power packed, life changing, mountain moving audio series can help you accelerate the journey on your road to success. Each tape in the series focuses on specific qualities and characteristics of success designed to enhance the whole person. In this series you will learn how to renew your mind so that you attract the things you want out of life instead of what you do not want.
Some of the titles in the Series include:

STA   How To Take Immediate Control of Your Destiny

STB   How to Get From Where You Are To Where
        You Want To Be

STC   The Power Of the Spoken Word

STD   The Fundamental Laws that Guarantee Success

STE   Inner Qualities of Success I
        (Commitment & Persistence)

STF   Inner Qualities of Success II
        (Gratitude & Enthusiasm) Regular $9.95 each

Special Offer Buy 3 Get 1 FREE

(#3) "Success: It's Your Birthright Action Guide"
If you like the ideas and concepts shared in the book you'll love this action guide. In it you'll find out what your life's mission is by going through our mission clarification workshop. You'll learn how to discover your hidden treasures, plus we'll show you how to create your own personal success conditioning audio tape and much more.

Regular $19.95 . . . Special Offer $14.95 *(with the purchase of any combination of items #1, #2 or #3).*

Order Form

Quantity	Description	Unit Price	Total Cost

Subtotal	_____
Taxes (MD residents 5%)	_____
Shipping $2.00 plus $1.00 for each additional item	_____
Total	_____

Please send my order to:

Please print clearly

_____ Check here if you want to be on mailing list.

Name: _____

Address: _____

_____

City: _____

State: _____ Zip: _____

Daytime Phone: _____

Evening Phone: _____

Please send check or money order to:

The Life Enrichment Institute
P.O Box 529,
Burtonsville, MD 20866
301-890-3405

If you are interested in obtaining any of the books listed at the end of the chapters contact your local bookstore or write:

The Life Enrichment Institute at
P.O. Box 529
Burtonsville, MD 20866
301-890-3405

For Quantity Discounts *Of Success: It's Your Birthright* and other life enriching books contact:

The Life Enrichment Institute
301-890-3405

Order Form

To order *Success: It's Your Birthright . . .*

Quantity	Description	Unit Price	Total Cost
		Subtotal	_____
	Taxes (MD residents 5%)		_____
		Shipping	_____
		Total	_____

Credit Card orders ONLY 1-800-444-2524

For Postal orders (Checks and Money orders) send $12.95 + $4.00 shipping ($1.00 shipping for each additional book) to:

**The Life Enrichment Institute
P.O. Box 529
Burtonsville, MD 20866**

Order Form

To order *Success: It's Your Birthright . . .*

Quantity	Description	Unit Price	Total Cost

Subtotal	_____
Taxes (MD residents 5%)	_____
Shipping	_____
Total	_____

Credit Card orders ONLY 1-800-444-2524

**For Postal orders (Checks and Money orders) send
$12.95 + $4.00 shipping ($1.00 shipping for each
additional book) to:**

**The Life Enrichment Institute
P.O. Box 529
Burtonsville, MD 20866**

How To Get Your Worldprofit Web Site or Your Own Domain Today!

1 To start your account, mail/fax this order form and payment to Worldprofit, Inc., Suite 208, 9010-106 Ave., Edmonton, Alberta, T5H 4K3, Canada. Fax (403) 425-6049.

2 To get your Home Page materials to us, either fax your camera-ready copy to us at (403) 425-6049, mail to the address at right, or e-mail webmaster@worldprofit.com (IBM files only).

3 To get your domain, just fill out the order form below and choose the domain name you would like.

If you need copywriting assistance, we can arrange it for you. We have professional copywriters standing by.

If you have also selected the Fax on Demand service, mail your documents flat (maximum of 3) to Worldprofit at the above address.

MALL SELECTION (Please select the Mall of your choice) — Additional Mall selections are $50 each per year.

❑ MONEY MALL
❑ BUSINESS TO BUSINESS MALL
❑ NETWORK MARKETING MALL
❑ HOME-BASED BUSINESS MALL
❑ INFOMALL

❑ BETTER HEALTH MALL
❑ MAIL ORDER MALL
❑ TOTAL HOME & GARDEN MALL
❑ GIFTS MALL
❑ CHRISTIAN MALL

PAYMENT OPTIONS (Please Note: All Prices in US Dollars)

❑ **OPTION 1:** I want my Home Page to run for six months. Enclosed is $129.95.

❑ **OPTION 2:** I want my Home Page to run for six months and profit from the Fax on Demand service. $189.95.

❑ **OPTION 3:** I want my Home Page to run for twelve months and receive a FREE 60 character ad on the "InternetConnect" card (circulation 100,000; $90 value) $199.95.

❑ **COPYWRITING SERVICE:** $79.95 per page. (You must call to arrange.)

Write the domain name you want:
http://www. _____
(Domain name registration subject to availability.)

❑ **DELUXE OPTION:** I want my Home Page to run for twelve months and profit from the Fax on Demand service. $329.95. YOU SAVE $139.95!

❑ **DOMAIN OPTION:** I want my own domain/virtual server for one year. $899.95. (Note: Price does not include a $100 registration fee to InterNic. They will bill you directly.)

❑ **LINK OPTION:** I want a link to my existing home page for one year. My URL address is http:// _____ . $199.95 (All links subject to Worldprofit, Inc. approval.)

❑ I would like additional info on Worldprofit maintaining my domain.

REMEMBER, YOUR WEB SITE CAN BE AS LARGE AS YOU WANT.
If you are uncertain about the cost, call (403) 425-2466 for assistance.

I would like to enhance my Home Page with these optional features:

❑ Extra Page(s) – $20 each
❑ Order Form – $25
❑ Color & Features Pkg – $25
❑ Color Picture(s) – $40 each
❑ Color Background – $10

Please send your check or money order (make payable to Worldprofit, Inc.) to:

Worldprofit, Inc.
Suite 208
9010-106 Ave Edmonton
Alberta, T5H 4K3, Canada
Ph: (403) 425-2466
or Fax: (403) 425-6049

For Faster Service, fax application & credit card info to (403) 425-6049.

Any questions? Call, fax, or e-mail Mgr. George Kosch.

❑ Check ❑ Money Order ❑ MC/Visa

Card # _____

Expiration Date _____

Signature _____

Name _____

Company _____

Address _____

City _____

State/Prov _____

Zip/PC _____

Phone ( ) _____

Fax ( ) _____

E-mail address _____

Note: No advertisements of a sexual or offensive nature will be accepted.

Your Dealer is: 5179

Free Vacation Accommodations!!!

Get **FREE** Vacation Accommodations to your choice of . . .

Hawaii, Mexico, Las Vegas, or Orlando

when you take advantage of our

SPECIAL BARGAIN.

Remember the dreams of traveling around the world you always had? Remember how exciting and beautiful everything was? Well, it's about to be that way again.

<u>YOUR DREAM HOLIDAY VACATION</u>

You're just a few weeks away from enjoying the vacation of your dreams that you have always imagined. In fact you're less than a few weeks away from taking the ideal vacation of your choice.

Imagine!!!

Picture yourself doing the Hula Hula dance on the beautiful and fabulous beaches of Waikiki, Hawaii. Relax in the sun of your choice of Acapulco, Puerto Vallarta or Mazatlan Mexico. Dance until dawn in exciting fun filled Las Vegas. Or just enjoy the calm blue waters and beautiful palm trees in Orlando, Florida where you can experience Disneyland and so much more.

Limited Time Offer

Because of your willingness to improve yourself financially, physically, emotionally, spiritually, etc., we have decided to make you a limited time offer you can't refuse. If you like the principles and ideas shared in this book, *"Success: It's Your Birthright,"* you're probably thinking of a few friends, relatives, co-workers or associates whose lives will be enhanced and enriched by this book. If you're like most generous and committed people, you're probably also thinking about taking the initiative to see that these same people get the book in their possession ASAP.

Well, we've decided to help you do just that. All you need to do is to send us the names of your friends (minimum three) and place an order for three additional copies of *"Success: It's Your Birthright"* (book ($12.95 each) or audio tapes ($9.95 each) or a combination of them), and we'll autograph them personally to your friends etc. Plus we'll also send you your certificate for your **FREE Vacation Accommodations to your choice of Hawaii, Mexico, Las Vegas, or Orlando.**

Limit: A maximum of four vacation certificates per person
(12 items ordered)

P.S. All orders must be sent directly to:

**The Life Enrichment Institute
P.O. Box 529
Burtonsville, MD 20866**

See order form on pages 139 & 140
100% Satisfaction Guaranteed or your Money Back